Bodies and Souls, or Spirited Bodies?

Are humans composed of a body and a nonmaterial mind or soul, or are we purely physical beings? Opinion is sharply divided over this issue. In this clear and concise book, Nancey Murphy argues for a physicalist account, but one that does not diminish traditional views of humans as rational, moral, and capable of relating to God. This position is motivated not only by developments in science and philosophy, but also by biblical studies and Christian theology. The reader is invited to appreciate the ways in which organisms are more than the sum of their parts, and that higher human capacities such as morality, free will, and religious awareness emerge from our neurobiological complexity and develop through our relation to others, to our cultural inheritance, and, most importantly, to God. Murphy addresses the questions of human uniqueness, religious experience, and personal identity before and after bodily resurrection.

NANCEY MURPHY is Professor of Christian Philosophy at Fuller Theological Seminary. She is an internationally known author and speaker in the field of religion and science. Professor Murphy's many publications include *Theology in the Age of Scientific Reasoning* (1990) and *Religion and Science: God, Evolution and the Soul* (2002).

CURRENT ISSUES IN THEOLOGY

General Editor

Iain Torrance
*Professor in Patristics and Christian Ethics, Master of Christ's College, and
Dean of the Faculty of Arts and Divinity, University of Aberdeen*

Editorial Advisory Board

David Ford *University of Cambridge*
Bryan Spinks *Yale University*
Kathryn Tanner *University of Chicago*
John Webster *University of Aberdeen*

There is a need among upper-undergraduate and graduate students of
theology, as well as among Christian teachers and church professionals, for a
series of short, focused studies of particular key topics in theology written by
prominent theologians. *Current Issues in Theology* meets this need.

The books in the series are designed to provide a 'state-of-the-art' statement
on the topic in question, engaging with contemporary thinking as well as
providing original insights. The aim is to publish books which stand between
the static monograph genre and the more immediate statement of a journal
article, by authors who are questioning existing paradigms or rethinking
perspectives.

Other titles in the series:

Holy Scripture: A Dogmatic Sketch John Webster
The Just War Revisited Oliver O'Donovan

Bodies and Souls,
or Spirited Bodies?

NANCEY MURPHY

CAMBRIDGE
UNIVERSITY PRESS

CAMBRIDGE UNIVERSITY PRESS
Cambridge, New York, Melbourne, Madrid, Cape Town, Singapore, São Paulo

Cambridge University Press
The Edinburgh Building, Cambridge CB2 8RU, UK

Published in the United States of America by Cambridge University Press, New York

www.cambridge.org
Information on this title: www.cambridge.org/9780521676762

First published 2006
Third printing 2007

Printed in the United Kingdom at the University Press, Cambridge

A catalogue record for this publication is available from the British Library

ISBN 978-0-521-85944-8 hardback
ISBN 978-0-521-67676-2 paperback

To my husband, Shel Rosell
forever, and then some

Contents

Figures

Preface

It is a strange fact about our culture that we are operating with a variety of radically different views of the basic nature of human beings. Even stranger is the fact that so few people seem to notice the first fact. Are humans immortal souls temporarily housed in physical bodies, or *are* we our bodies? The purpose of this book is to pursue this question from the perspectives of three disciplines: Christian theology, science (especially the cognitive neurosciences), and philosophy.

My central thesis is, first, that we are our bodies – there is no additional metaphysical element such as a mind or soul or spirit. But, second, this "physicalist" position need not deny that we are intelligent, moral, and spiritual. We are, at our best, complex physical organisms, imbued with the legacy of thousands of years of culture, and, most importantly, blown by the Breath of God's Spirit; we are *Spirited bodies*.

This book has grown almost organically, rather than in the linear manner of most books. It began as a single lecture, variations of which I have been privileged to present at numerous institutions as distant as New Zealand and South Africa. It divided in half and each half grew when I was invited to give the Harold Stoner Clark Lectures at California Lutheran University in Thousand Oaks, California. The invitation to give a series of three lectures at General Theological Seminary in New York led to further division and growth, finally culminating in its four-part structure when I gave the Scottish Journal of Theology Lectures at the University of Aberdeen. I have profited immensely from discussion at all of these institutions.

I have also enjoyed the hospitality of Professor Mitties DeChamplain at GTS, along with that of her husband Ron, recently deceased. Iain Torrance was responsible for inviting me to give the SJT Lectures; he and his wife Morag offered me lodging in the guest apartment of their centuries-old farmhouse, showed me castles, and introduced me to the adventures of Scottish dining. Thank you all so much!

Thanks also to students at Fuller Seminary who have read drafts of the book and have given me valuable suggestions for improvement. Also deep gratitude to my colleague at Fuller, Warren Brown. He and I have been working on the philosophical and scientific issues touched upon in this book for the past five years. Philosophers will not be satisfied with the arguments herein against neurobiological reductionism. Neither are we; we hope soon to publish an adequate treatment of the issue.

In its process of growth this book has incorporated pieces written for other purposes. Several pages are adapted from *In Search of the Soul*, edited by Joel B. Green and Stuart L. Palmer, copyright 2005 by Joel B. Green and Stuart L. Palmer, used with permission of InterVarsity Press, P. O. Box 1400, Downers Grove, IL 60515, www.ivpress.com. Others are adapted from *Whatever Happened to the Soul?* edited by Warren S. Brown, Nancey Murphy, and H. Newton Malony, copyright 1998, used with permission of Augsburg-Fortress Press, P. O. Box 1209, Minneapolis, MN 55440.

1 | Do Christians need souls? Theological and biblical perspectives on human nature

1. Prospect and problems

One thing we have in common with the first Christians is this: we have available to us a wealth of conflicting ideas about what a human being, most basically, is. It is important to be aware of this fact since whatever we believe on this subject will influence how we think about a great number of other issues, for example: What happens to us after we die? Is an embryo a person? Ordinarily we do not discuss our theories of human nature, so these disagreements are kept largely below the surface of our debates. Here is an example: when Dolly the sheep was cloned I received calls from media people looking for a Christian reaction. One reporter seemed frustrated that I had no strong condemnation of the idea of cloning humans. After his repeated attempts to provoke me to express some sort of horror at the prospect, light dawned for me. I asked him, "Do you read a lot of science fiction?" "Well, some." "Are you imagining that if we try to clone a human being we'll clone a body but it won't have a soul? It will be like the zombies in science fiction?" "Yes, something like that." "Well," I said, "don't worry. None of us has a soul and we all get along perfectly well!"

Because we seldom discuss our theories of human nature it is difficult to know what others think. I have had to resort to informal polling whenever I get the chance. I ask students in various classes and often ask my audiences when I lecture. Here are some options. The first can be called either physicalism or materialism. This is the view that humans are composed of only one "part," a physical body. The terms "physicalism" and "materialism" are nearly interchangeable in philosophy but "physicalism" is more fashionable now, and it is more appealing to Christians because "materialism" has long been used to refer to a *worldview* that excludes the divine. So even though a materialist account of the person is perfectly compatible with belief in God, "materialism" does carry those unhappy connotations for Christians.

The second option is dualism, and we recognize two sorts these days, body–soul and body–mind dualism. The terms "mind" and "soul" were once (nearly) interchangeable, but in recent years "soul" has taken on religious connotations that "mind" has not.

A third theory regarding the composition of human beings is called trichotomism. This view comes from Paul's blessing in 1 Thessalonians 5:23 (NRSV): "May the God of peace himself sanctify you entirely; and may your spirit and soul and body be kept blameless at the coming of the Lord Jesus Christ." So trichotomists hold that humans are composed of three parts: body, soul, and spirit.

I believe that these are the main competitors today, but another view has been important in the past. This view is also monistic, as is physicalism, in holding that humans are made of only one kind of substance, but here the whole is resolved into the spiritual or mental. This was an important position in earlier centuries when idealism was popular in philosophy. Idealism is the metaphysical thesis that all of reality is essentially mental. I understand that some New Age thinkers have similar views. I'll call this view idealist monism.

Here is the quiz:

Which of the following comes closest to your understanding of human nature?

1. Humans are composed of one "part": a physical body (materialism/physicalism).
2. Humans are composed of two parts:
   2a. A body and a soul.
   2b. A body and a mind (dualism).

3. Humans are composed of three parts: body, soul, and spirit (trichotomism).
4. Humans are composed of one "part": a spiritual/mental substance (idealism).
5. Who cares?

The results I usually get are as follows: among my Evangelical students at Fuller Theological Seminary, as well as with a general audience, dualism and trichotomism compete for first place. There are usually only one or two physicalists and one or two idealists. In groups of specialists the numbers are quite different. If I were to ask scientists, I am sure I would find that most biologists and especially neuroscientists are physicalists. However, it is not so easy to predict what chemists or physicists will say. Answers here are related to the issue of reductionism, which I shall address throughout this volume. If I ask philosophers, their answers will depend largely on whether they are Christians or not. Secular philosophers are almost all physicalists – I only know one exception.[1] Christian philosophers are divided between dualism and physicalism. When I speak at seminaries on the liberal end of the spectrum all but incoming students are physicalists. At more conservative institutions faculty members are split between dualism and physicalism. Item 5, "Who cares?" is included at a teaser, since I shall argue that it actually represents the biblical view.

My quiz and category system make it appear that there is agreement at least to the extent of our having only four theories. But if one asks individuals what they mean by "soul" or "spirit" or even by the word "physical" one gets almost as many different answers as there are people! I read a recent book review claiming that 130 different views of the human person have been

---

[1] This is William D. Hart, who delivered a lecture titled "Unity and dualism" at a symposium on mind and body at Westmont College, Santa Barbara, CA on February 15, 2002.

documented.[2] Why do we agree so little about something so important? Much of this has to do with the fact that a number of different disciplines have an influence here – science, philosophy, and theology – and each has contributed to changing views over the centuries. Another important factor, I shall argue, is the fact that *the Bible has no clear teaching here*. This has made it possible for Christians in different eras to recognize a variety of views in the texts, and, perhaps more importantly, to have read a variety of views *into* the texts.

My plan for this volume, then, is to examine in this first chapter the biblical and theological issues, but the theological story cannot be told without some attention to ancient philosophy. The history is complex: there have been a number of changes in what Christians have believed over the years, but this is complicated by conflicting views among historians *about* what Christians have believed over the years. There seems to be no other enquiry into which we humans are more likely to project our own views. So I shall begin with recent historiographical disputes, and then, armed with a good dose of suspicion, I shall go back to look, first, at the philosophies that contributed to the development of doctrine and then to the Bible itself. I shall end with some attention to the implications of a physicalist anthropology for systematic theology, and some recommendations for Christian spiritual formation.

In my second chapter I shall concentrate on the scientific issues. Here I shall examine the impact of three developments: the introduction of atomism in early modern physics, the Darwinian revolution, and, finally, current developments in the cognitive neurosciences. A significant consequence of modern physics was to create what is now seen to be an insuperable problem for dualists: mind–body interaction. Evolutionary theory, with its

---

[2] Review by Graham McFarlane of N. H. Gregersen *et al.*, eds., *The Human Person in Science and Theology* (Edinburgh: T. & T. Clark, 2000), in *Science and Christian Belief* 14, no. 1 (April 2002): 94–5.

emphasis on our continuity with animals, raised the question of how it could be that we have souls while the (other) animals do not. The significance of contemporary neuroscience is this: all of the capacities once attributed to the mind or soul now appear to be (largely) functions of the brain.

In both of these first two chapters I shall be arguing either directly or indirectly for a physicalist account of human nature. However, physicalism has not been a predominant view in either philosophy or theology until recently. There are a number of philosophical problems that need to be addressed if physicalism is to be acceptable to Christians. In my third and fourth chapters, then, I shall alert you to the most significant of these problems and sketch out some rough indicators of where solutions might lie.

A central philosophical issue is reductionism, what neuropsychologist Donald MacKay called "nothing-buttery." The essential question is this: if humans are purely physical, then how can it *fail* to be the case that all of our thoughts and behavior are simply determined by the laws of neurobiology? In chapter 3, I first explain what is wrong with reductionism in general, and then sketch out an account of how our complex neural equipment, along with cultural resources, underlies our capacities for both morality and free will.

In chapter 4, I address a variety of other philosophical problems. One is simply the question of how we know physicalism is true. I argue that if it is treated as a scientific hypothesis rather than a philosophical doctrine we see that it has all of the confirming evidence one could hope for (much of it sketched in chapter 2).

The two remaining issues are related to the difference between reductionist and *non*-reductionist versions of physicalism. First, if humans have no souls, what accounts for the traditional view that we have a special place among the animals; in other words, in what does human distinctiveness lie? I shall focus on morality and the ability to be in relationship with God. I argue that our capacity for religious experience is enabled by culture and by our complex neural systems, just as is our capacity for morality. However, a relationship is two-sided; thus I next address the issue of how God relates to us if we are wholly a part of the physical order.

Finally there is the question: if there is no soul, what accounts for personal identity over time? More particularly, how can we say that the person after resurrection is the same person as before if the resurrection body is so different from the earthly body? I offer an account of personal identity in terms of the identity over time of the high-level capacities that our bodies enable: consciousness, memory, moral character, interpersonal relationships, and, especially, our relationship with God.

2. History's ambiguous message

When I first became interested in the topic of human nature I believed that a close look at the Bible and at the development of Christian theology could settle the issue of what Christians *ought* to believe about human nature. Surely I could grab a book from the library that traced the history of this issue. So far I have failed to find one. Since I am not competent to do primary research in either early church history or biblical studies, I turned to secondary sources in order to try to put together my own account. I was further frustrated to find very little on this topic in histories of early Christian thought.

My next resort was to reference works, both theological and biblical. I looked up relevant words such as "body," "soul," "spirit," "immortality," and "resurrection." I discovered something interesting: the views attributed to biblical authors varied considerably from one source to another. I came to the conclusion that they were a better indicator of the views *assumed* in the era in which they were written than of what the biblical authors actually believed. So one important part of the history of these ideas needs to be an account of the *oversimplifications* and even falsifications of earlier history.

Further complications in recent history are the differences between Protestant and Catholic views, and especially between liberal and conservative Protestants. My conclusion is that to do justice to this topic one would have to write not a single book, but a series of volumes. So what can I write in one short chapter that does not contribute to the history of oversimplifications of history? Rather than telling the story from beginning to end, I shall begin with some of the twists and turns in biblical criticism and history of doctrine in recent centuries.

There seem to be only three points in Christian history when teaching about the metaphysical composition of the person has become a focal point. The first was when Christianity spread from a largely Hebraic context to the surrounding Mediterranean world. The second was during the Aristotelian revival in the middle ages, occasioned by Islamic scholars' presence in Europe. The third was a response to the rise of biblical criticism and critical church history in the modern era. Critical church history provided modern thinkers with a sense of the historical development of doctrine, which allowed questions to arise in a new way about the consistency of later church teachings with those of the Bible.

2.1 Contradictions in historical criticism

Historical criticism of the Bible itself has had a major impact on modern conceptions of the person, but there have been *contradictory tendencies*. Notice that Christians have two strikingly different conceptions of what happens after we die. One is based on dualism: the body dies and the soul departs to be with God. The other is the expectation of bodily resurrection. For centuries these two ideas have been combined. The body dies, the soul departs, and at the end of time the soul receives a resurrected or transformed body. Biblical scholarship has teased out these two ideas, immortality versus resurrection.

In the eighteenth and especially the nineteenth centuries many New Testament scholars cast doubt on the historicity of miracles in general and the great miracle of Jesus' resurrection in particular. Skepticism about Jesus' resurrection led to increased emphasis among theologians on the immortality of the soul as the only basis for Christian hope in an afterlife. Philosophy was important here as well. Immanuel Kant (1724–1804) has been the most influ-ential philosopher in the development of liberal theology. He devised a "transcendental" argument for the soul's immortality, which nicely reinforced the tendency among theologians to see body–soul dualism as the "Enlightened" Christian position. Consider Adolf von Harnack's neat summary of the kernel of Christian doctrine: the fatherhood of God, the brotherhood of man, and the infinite value of the human *soul*.[3]

Meanwhile – and here is the contradictory tendency – biblical scholars had begun to question whether body–soul dualism was in fact the position to be found in Scripture. One important contribu-tion here was the work of H. Wheeler Robinson, an Old Testament scholar whose book, *The Christian Doctrine of Man*, went through three editions and eight printings between 1911 and 1952.[4] Robinson argued that the Hebrew idea of personality is that of an animated body, not (like the Greek) that of an incarnated soul. However, while arguing that the New Testament is largely continuous with the Old in conceiving of the person as a unity rather than dualistically, he also said that the most important advance in the New Testament is the belief that the essential personality (whether called the *psyche* or the *pneuma*) survives bodily death. This soul or spirit may be temporarily disembodied, but it is not complete without the body, and its

---

[3] Adolf von Harnack, *Das Wesen des Christentums* (1900); translated as *What is Christianity?* (1901).

[4] H. Wheeler Robinson, *The Christian Doctrine of Man* (Edinburgh: T. & T. Clark, 1911). While Robinson's account of Old Testament teaching struck a blow against dualism, it did not support physicalism directly since Robinson interpreted theories of human nature in terms of his idealist philosophy.

continued existence after bodily death is dependent upon God rather than a natural endowment of the soul. So here we see the beginning of the recognition that dualism was not the original Hebraic understanding. He sees a modified dualism as a New Testament invention.

Theological thinking on these issues around the time Robinson wrote can only be described as confused. This can be seen by comparing related entries in reference works from early in the twentieth century. In *The New Schaff-Herzog Encyclopedia of Religious Knowledge* (1910) there is a clear consensus that the whole of the Bible is dualistic.[5] The general understanding was that the human soul is bound to corporeality in this life, yet it survives death because it possesses the Spirit of God. Resurrection is understood as God's giving new bodies to souls that have rested in God since the death of the old body.

Yet in a slightly earlier work, *A Dictionary of the Bible* (1902), two sharply opposed views appear.[6] An article on "Soul" says that throughout most of the Bible, the terms usually translated as "soul" such as the Hebrew word *nephesh* or the Greek *psyche* do *not* in fact refer to a substantial soul. Instead they are simply equivalent to the *life* embodied in living creatures (4:608). The article on "Resurrection," however, subscribes to body–soul dualism. Resurrection is described as "the clothing of the soul with a body" (4:236). So some of the authors in this dictionary assume dualism while others explicitly deny that it is the anthropology of the Bible.

This tendency to juxtapose incompatible accounts of biblical teaching continued through the middle of the twentieth century, when several new factors gave the issue greater prominence. One was the rise of neo-orthodox theology after World War I. Karl Barth and others made a sharp distinction between Hebraic and Hellenistic conceptions, and strongly favored the former. Barth

---

[5] Samuel Macauley Jackson, ed. (New York and London: Funk and Wagnalls Company, 1910).

[6] James Hastings, ed. (Edinburgh: T. & T. Clark, 1902).

also argued for the centrality of the resurrection in Christian teaching. The biblical theology movement in the mid-twentieth century continued to press for the restoration of earlier, Hebraic understandings of Christianity.

A decisive contribution was Rudolf Bultmann's claim in his *Theology of the New Testament* that Paul uses *sōma* ("body") to characterize the human person as a whole.[7] In 1955 Oscar Cullmann gave the lectures that were published as *Immortality of the Soul or Resurrection of the Dead: The Witness of the New Testament*. Here Cullman drew out the contrast between biblical attitudes toward death, along with expectation of bodily resurrection, and Socrates' attitude given his expectation that his soul would survive the death of his body.[8]

2.2 So where do we stand?

A survey of the literature of theology and biblical studies throughout the twentieth century, then, shows a gradual displacement of a dualistic account of the person, with its correlative emphasis on the afterlife conceived in terms of the immortality of the soul. First there was the recognition of the holistic character of biblical conceptions of the person, often while still presupposing temporarily separable "parts." Later there developed a holistic *but also physicalist* account of the person, combined with an emphasis on bodily resurrection. One way of highlighting this shift is to note that in *The Encyclopedia of Religion and Ethics* (published between 1909 and 1921) there is a lengthy article on "Soul" and no entry for "Resurrection."[9] In *The Anchor Bible Dictionary* (published in 1992) there is no entry at all for "Soul" but a very long set of articles on "Resurrection"![10]

---

[7] Rudolf Bultmann, *Theology of the New Testament*, vol. 1 (New York: Scribner, 1951).

[8] Oscar Cullmann, *Immortality of the Soul or Resurrection of the Dead?* (New York: Macmillan, 1958).

[9] James Hastings, ed. (New York: Charles Scribner's Sons, 1909–21).

[10] David Noel Freedman, ed. (New York: Doubleday, 1992).

So has critical scholarship settled this issue? The foregoing picture of twentieth-century thought is an oversimplification for three reasons. First, the twentieth century has seen the development in American Protestantism of two distinct theological traditions. The account given above traces developments in what we may loosely call the liberal tradition. Meanwhile, however, the tendency among conservatives has been to maintain a dualist account of the person.

A second complication is Catholic thought. There is little difference between Catholic and Protestant biblical scholarship, but considerable difference between (official) Catholic theology and that of Protestant thinkers. I shall say a bit more about Catholic thought further on in this chapter.

Finally, it has turned out that the distinction between Hellenistic and Hebraic thought is not as sharp as has been supposed. Not all Greek thinkers were dualists, and dualism had already arisen as one option within Jewish thought several centuries before Christ.[11] So let us look at Greek and Roman philosophy and its influence on early Christian theology.[12]

3. Ancient philosophy and early Christian thought

It has become common to associate ancient philosophers with something like modern Cartesian dualism, but this is an over-simplification, first, as already mentioned, because the philosophers of Greece and Rome were not at all united on these issues.

---

[11] See Joel B. Green, "'Bodies – That is, Human Lives': A Re-examination of Human Nature in the Bible," in Warren S. Brown, Nancey Murphy, and H. Newton Malony, eds., *Whatever Happened to the Soul? Scientific and Theological Portraits of Human Nature* (Minneapolis: Fortress Press, 1998), 149–73; and Neil Gillman, *The Death of Death: Resurrection and Immortality in Jewish Thought* (Woodstock, VT: Jewish Lights Publishing, 1997).

[12] This section and the following draw upon material from my "Human Nature: Historical, Scientific, and Religious Issues," in Brown *et al.*, eds., *Whatever Happened to the Soul?*, 1–29.

Second, it is difficult to think our way back to these ancient sources; we have a fairly precise concept of the material, which allows for a sharp distinction between the material and the non-material. However, one of the contentious issues in ancient philosophy was the nature of matter itself. For many Greek thinkers, reality was conceived of as a hierarchy of beings exhibiting varying degrees of materiality. One important question in ancient philosophy was whether or not the soul belonged to this gradation of material realities. The stoics regarded the human soul as but an aspect of an all-pervading cosmic logos, but Epicureans provided an atomist–materialist account of the soul.

3.1 Plato and Aristotle

The two philosophers who have had the greatest impact on Christian theology are Plato and Aristotle. While Plato's account is indeed dualistic, it is not clear that Aristotle's account should be so regarded. Plato (427?–348 BCE) described the person as an immortal soul imprisoned in a mortal body. The soul is tripartite and hierarchically organized. There is an analogy between the harmonious functioning of the soul and that of the ideal city-state. The appetitive or impulsive element of the soul is analogous to the lowest class in society, the consumers. Reason is the highest element, and corresponds to the ruling class. In between is an element corresponding to the soldier-police. The name for this element, *thumos*, may be translated "spirit" but in the sense in which a horse has spirit. The proper coordination of these three elements or faculties constitutes human well-being.

Plato's concept of the soul was related to his "other-worldly" view of reality. During much of his career he held the doctrine of the *forms* or *ideas* – the view that concepts have a real existence and are eternal. He argued from the fact that people possess knowledge of these forms without being taught that they must have come to know them by acquaintance before birth. Thus, the rational part of the soul pre-exists the body, dwelling in the transcendent realm of the forms, and returns there at death.

In his mature position, Plato's student Aristotle (384–22 BCE) thought of the soul not as an entity, but more as a life principle – that aspect of the person which provides the powers or attributes characteristic of the human being. Plants and animals have souls as well – nutritive and sensitive souls, which give them the powers to grow and reproduce and to move and perceive, respectively. Human souls are organized hierarchically and incorporate the nutritive and sensitive powers, but in addition provide rational powers. He illustrates the relation of soul to body with an analogy: if the eye were a complete animal, sight would be its soul. Because the soul is a principle of the functioning of the body, it would follow that the soul dies with the body. However, a vestige of Aristotle's earlier, Platonic dualism remains in his speculation that perhaps one aspect of rationality (*nous*) survives death. But even if this is the case, this does not amount to personal immortality, since *nous* is an impersonal rational faculty.

Aristotle's conception of the soul and body fits well into his general "hylomorphic" conception of reality. All material things are composed of matter and form. Form is an immanent principle that gives things their essential characteristics and powers. The soul is but one type of form. Although Aristotle uses the same term ("form") as Plato, it is important to stress the differences between their views. Aristotle's forms are not pre-existent, transcendent entities, as for Plato. Since for Aristotle the soul is a form, this difference matters a great deal in his concept of the person, and makes it questionable whether Aristotle's view should be considered an instance of body–soul dual*ism* at all. We shall come back to Aristotelian physics in the next chapter.

3.2 Early Christian responses

It is true that early Christian theologians developed their accounts of human nature in conversation with Hellenistic philosophers, yet given the diversity of philosophical views, there came to be equally diverse accounts among early Christian thinkers. Tertullian (160–220) followed the Stoics in teaching that the human soul is corporeal and is generated with the body. Origen (185–254) followed Plato in teaching that the soul is incorporeal and eternal, pre-existing the body. After the time of Jerome (c. 347–420) the soul was generally thought to be created at the time of conception.

Augustine (354–430) has been the most influential teacher on these matters because of his legacy in both Protestant and Catholic theology and because of his importance in the development of Christian spirituality. Augustine's conception of the person is a modified Platonic view: a human being is an immortal (not eternal) soul using (not imprisoned in) a mortal body. The soul is tripartite and hierarchically ordered. However, the "parts" are slightly different from those recognized by Plato. Our modern conception of the will is an Augustinian invention and for Augustine the will is superior to the intellect, and both are superior to the appetites.

Augustine was much influenced by the Neoplatonists, who had incorporated Platonic philosophy into religious systems emphasizing the care and development of the soul as the means of salvation. Augustine bequeathed this emphasis on the soul to subsequent spiritual writers. It is by cultivating the higher faculties of the soul (and often by repressing the lower faculties and the body) that one develops the capacity for knowledge of and relation to God.

3.3 Medieval and Reformation developments

I now "fast-forward" my historical narrative from Augustine, writing in late antiquity, to Thomas Aquinas, the greatest of medieval synthesists. Thomas (1225–74) provided an Aristotelian alternative to Augustine's Platonism. Thomas took up Aristotle's hylomorphic metaphysics as well as his thesis that the soul is the form of the body. He also benefited considerably in his work from Islamic scholars and their commentaries on Aristotle.

Thomas had an elaborate account of the hierarchically ordered faculties or powers of the soul. The "lowest" powers of the human soul, shared with plants and animals, are the vegetative faculties of nutrition, growth, and reproduction. Next higher are the sensitive faculties, shared with animals. These include the exterior senses of sight, hearing, smell, taste, and touch. He also recognized four "interior senses," for example, the *vis aestimativa*. This estimative power is the ability to recognize that something is useful or useless, friendly or unfriendly. The sensitive level of the soul also provides for the power of locomotion and for lower aspects of appetite – that is, the ability to be attracted to sensible objects – and for eleven kinds of emotion: love, desire, delight, hate, aversion, sorrow, fear, daring, hope, despair, and anger.

The rational faculties are distinctively human: passive and active intellect, and will. The will is a higher appetitive faculty whose object is the good. Since God is ultimate goodness, this faculty is ultimately directed toward God. Morality is a function of attraction to the good combined with rational judgment as to what the good truly consists in.

Given the vagueness of many current accounts of the soul, Thomas provides a high-water mark for both clarity and specificity. When we consider scientific developments in the next chapter it will be important to remember that *all* of these cognitive and emotional capacities were once attributed to the soul. Thomas's account continues to be important today, as well, because it is still influential in Catholic thought.

I now fast-forward again, to the Protestant Reformation. The Reformation, for all its repercussions elsewhere in theology, seems not to have brought the issue of human nature to the forefront, except for a controversy over the "intermediate state," that is, the question of whether the soul enjoys conscious awareness of God between death and the resurrection of the body. This issue became prominent during the Reformation in connection with controversies over purgatory and the expectation of the imminent return of Christ. The problem is that if there is no substantial soul to survive bodily death then what is to be made of this doctrine? Martin Luther and other reformers, especially within the radical wing, argued that the soul "sleeps" prior to the resurrection and the Last Judgment. Since "sleep" is a euphemism in the New Testament for death, there are actually two possibilities here – that the soul actually dies with the body or that it is, in some sense, asleep. Some, such as the Polish Anabaptist Simon Budny, taught the more radical view that the soul is but the life of the body and thus ceases to exist at death. More commonly, the radicals taught that the soul continues to exist, yet in an unconscious state.[13]

John Calvin attacked both sorts of views, beginning with a treatise called *Psychopannychia* (1545). This word means a watchful or sentient "wake" of the soul, but nonetheless has come to be associated instead with the two positions Calvin was opposing.[14] Calvin's teaching on the conscious intermediate state has settled this issue for many of his followers. The same teaching had been made official for Catholicism by the Fifth Lateran council in 1513. Thus, the doctrine of the "intermediate state" still serves as a motive for body–soul dualism among some conservative Christians, both Catholic and Reformed.

4. So what *does* the Bible say?

I ended section 2 with a report on the mid-twentieth-century conclusion that the Bible teaches a holistic view somewhat like contemporary physicalism and that dualism came into Christian teaching only later under the influence of Greek and Roman philosophy. We have seen that most Christian theology has in fact been greatly influenced by Hellenistic philosophy, but those influences were various.

---

[13] John Hunston Williams, *The Radical Reformation* (Philadelphia: Westminster Press, 1962), chapter 23.

[14] Ibid., 581.

Being a proponent of physicalism, and teaching at a seminary where biblical authority is paramount, I would like to be able to state unequivocally that physicalism is the position of the Bible. Unfortunately (for me) it is more complicated than that. While there is wide agreement among biblical scholars that at least the earlier Hebraic scriptures know nothing of body–soul dualism, it is surprisingly difficult to settle the issue of what the New Testament has to say.

4.1 Old Testament scholarship

Let us consider first the Old Testament. If current scholars are correct in their claim that the original Hebraic conception of the person comes closer to current physicalist accounts than to body–soul dualism, how could Christians have been wrong about this for so many centuries? Part of the answer involves translation. The Septuagint is a Greek translation of the Hebrew scriptures, probably dating from around 250 BCE. This text translated Hebrew anthropological terminology into Greek, and it then contained the terms that, in the minds of Christians influenced by Greek philosophy, referred to constituent parts of humans. Christians since then have obligingly read them and translated them in this way. The clearest instance of this is the Hebrew word *nephesh*, which was translated as *psyche* in the Septuagint and later translated into English as "soul." To illustrate, here are a few lines as they were translated in the King James Version:

> Psalm 16:10: "For thou wilt not leave my soul in Hell."
> Psalm 25:20: "O keep my soul and deliver me; let me not be ashamed."
> Psalm 26:9: "Gather not my soul with sinners."
> Psalm 49:14–15: "[They that trust in their wealth] like sheep they are laid in the grave; death shall feed on them – but God will redeem my soul from the power of the grave . . ."

These passages fit nicely with a view that, while the body may decay in the grave, God saves souls; this sounds exactly like body–soul dualism. Notice, though, that there are other references to the soul in the Hebrew scriptures that do not fit this dualist picture at all:

> Psalm 7:1–2: "O Lord my God in thee do I put my trust: save me from all them that persecute me . . . Lest he tear my soul like a lion, rending it in pieces."
> Psalm 22:20: "Deliver my soul from the sword."
> Psalm 35:7: ". . . without cause have they hid for me their net in a pit, which without cause they have digged for my soul."

These passages are strange in the old translations – it is bodies, not souls, that are torn or stabbed, and souls cannot be thrown into pits. Even a passage in Genesis that is often used to support dualism sounds odd. Genesis 2:7 used to read: "And the Lord God formed man of the dust of the ground and breathed into his nostrils the breath of life and man became a living soul." Should it not say instead, "God breathed a *soul* into his nostrils and he became a living *being*"?

It is widely agreed now that the Hebrew word translated "soul" in all these cases – *nephesh* – did not mean what later Christians have meant by "soul." In most of these cases, it is simply a way of referring to the whole living person. Here is how more recent versions translate some of these same passages:

> Psalm 16:10: (KJV) "For thou wilt not leave my soul in hell"; (REB) "for you will not abandon *me* to Sheol. . . ."
> Psalm 25:20: (KJV) "Oh keep my soul and deliver me"; (NIV) "Guard *my life* and rescue me."

The Genesis passage is translated as "man became a living being" (NIV) or "a living creature" (REB).

Biblical scholar Robert Gundry writes that ". . . we confront a current understanding of OT (Old Testament) anthropology by now so common that its maxims need no quotation marks. It is that in the OT body and soul do not contrast. Man is an animated body rather than an incarnated soul."[15] Yet Gundry (in the work just cited) is one of the most articulate proponents of a dualistic interpretation of the New Testament.

4.2 Conflicting accounts of the New Testament

The New Testament, being written in Greek, has also been read in light of Greek philosophy, and, in addition, there are a number of passages that many take to show that the New Testament authors espoused a dualist anthropology. These include: (1) Matthew 10:28 (REB), "Do not fear those who kill the body, but cannot kill the soul. Fear him rather who is able to destroy both soul and body in Hell;" (2) Luke 16:19–31, the story of Lazarus in which (without reference to prior resurrection of the body) Lazarus is said to be with Abraham; (3) Luke 23:39–43, in which Jesus says to one of those crucified with him that he will be with him today in Paradise; and (4) 2 Corinthians 5:1–10, in which Paul says that "in this present body we groan, yearning to be covered by our heavenly habitation put over this one, in the hope that, being thus clothed, we shall not find ourselves naked."

It is not clear what to make of these passages. For example, the Lukan parallel to the text from Matthew reads "do not fear those who kill the body and after that have nothing more they can do ... fear him who, after he has killed, has authority to cast into hell ..." (Lk. 12:4–5). Which is the better representation of Jesus' own words?

The other passages here are taken by some current scholars to allude to or presuppose a conscious intermediate state between death and the final resurrection. John W. Cooper, a philosophical theologian at Calvin Theological Seminary, published his book,

---

[15] Robert H. Gundry, *Sōma in Biblical Theology: With Emphasis on Pauline Anthropology* (Grand Rapids, MI: Zondervan Press, 1987), 119.

Body, Soul, and Life Everlasting in 1989.[16] Cooper gave a fine over-
view of scientific and theological challenges to dualism, yet argued
for a dualist position on the grounds that Scripture supports the
doctrine of the intermediate state, and the doctrine of the intermediate state necessarily presupposes dualism. Cooper bases his
argument on the concept of Sheol in the Old Testament and on a
variety of New Testament texts that he takes to refer to an intermediate state. Two recent and influential books rely on Cooper's
exegesis: one is William Hasker's *The Emergent Self*,[17] and the other
is J. P. Moreland and Scott B. Rae's *Body and Soul*.[18]

To illustrate the problems involved in taking these passages at
face value, consider New Testament scholar Joel Green's criticisms
of Cooper's arguments.[19] I will lay out Green's response to Luke
23:40–3, the report of Jesus' promise to the thief on the cross. The
important question here is whether Cooper is correct in taking
"Paradise" to refer to an intermediate resting place of the dead or
whether instead it refers to the *final* reward of the righteous. Cooper
argues his case on the basis of the meaning of "Paradise" in inter-
testamental, or Second Temple Jewish, writings. Cooper claims that
the term is usually applied to the intermediate state rather than to
the final abode of the righteous. Green contests this claim and
argues that Cooper's account shows "insufficient nuance with
regard to the nature and diversity of perspectives on death and the
afterlife represented in the literature of Second Temple Judaism."[20]

---

[16] John W. Cooper, *Body, Soul, and Life Everlasting: Biblical Anthropology and the
Monism–Dualism Debate* (Grand Rapids: Eerdmans, 1989, second enlarged edn.,
2000).

[17] William Hasker, *The Emergent Self* (Ithaca and London: Cornell University Press,
1999).

[18] J. P. Moreland and Scott B. Rae, *Body and Soul: Human Nature and the Crisis in Ethics*
(Downers Grove, IL: InterVarsity Press, 2000).

[19] Joel B. Green, "Eschatology and the Nature of Humans: A Reconsideration of
Pertinent Biblical Evidence," *Science and Christian Belief* 14, no. 1 (April 2002): 33–50.

[20] Ibid., 46.

My point in reporting this argument is not to take sides with one or the other, but rather to show the difficulty in determining what a New Testament author has in mind on this particular issue. My question is this: do Christians really need to work through a long list of non-Canonical books in order to determine what the Bible teaches on this issue? The unlikelihood of a positive answer to my rhetorical question leads me to this conclusion: the New Testament authors are not intending to teach *anything* about humans' metaphysical composition. If they were, surely they could have done so much more clearly!

Helpful support for this conclusion comes from New Testament scholar James Dunn. Dunn distinguishes between what he calls "aspective" and "partitive" accounts of human nature. Dunn writes:

> ... in simplified terms, while Greek thought tended to regard the human being as made up of distinct parts, Hebraic thought saw the human being more as a whole person existing on different dimensions. As we might say, it was more characteristically Greek to conceive of the human person "partitively," whereas it was more characteristically Hebrew to conceive of the human person "aspectively." That is to say, we speak of a school *having* a gym (the gym is part of the school); but we say I *am* a Scot (my Scottishness is an aspect of my whole being).[21]

So the Greek philosophers we have surveyed were interested in the question: what are the essential parts that make up a human being? In contrast, for the biblical authors each "part" ("part" in scare quotes) stands for the whole person thought of from a certain angle. For example, "spirit" stands for the whole person in relation to God. What the New Testament authors are concerned with, then, is human beings in relationship to the natural world, to the

---

[21] James D. G. Dunn, *The Theology of the Apostle Paul* (Grand Rapids, MI: Eerdmans, 1998), 54. Dunn attributes the aspective/partitive account to D. E. H. Whitely, *The Theology of St Paul* (Oxford: Blackwell, 1964).

community, and to God. Paul's distinction between spirit and flesh is not our later distinction between soul and body. Paul is concerned with two ways of living: one in conformity with the Spirit of God, and the other in conformity to the old aeon before Christ. Recall that item 5 in my survey (above) was "Who cares?" I included that option to represent Dunn's (widely shared) thesis regarding the apparent unimportance of our question about "parts" for the biblical authors.

4.3 My thesis

So I conclude that there is no such thing as *the* biblical view of human nature *insofar as we are interested in a partitive account*. The biblical authors, especially the New Testament authors, wrote within the context of a wide variety of views, probably as diverse as in our own day, but did not take a clear stand on one theory or another. What the New Testament authors *do* attest is, first, that humans are psychophysical unities; second, that Christian hope for eternal life is staked on bodily resurrection rather than an immortal soul; and, third, that humans are to be understood in terms of their relationships – relationships to the community of believers and especially to God.

I believe that we can conclude, further, that this leaves contemporary Christians free to choose among several options. It would be very bold of me to say that dualism *per se* is ruled out, given that it has been so prominent in the tradition. However, the radical dualisms of Plato and René Descartes,[22] which take the body to be unnecessary for, or even a hindrance to, full human life, are clearly out of bounds. Equally unacceptable is any physicalist account that denies human ability to be in relationship with God. Thus, many reductionist forms of physicalism are also out of bounds. More on this in chapters 3 and 4.

---

[22] I describe Descartes's position in chapter 2.

5. Physicalism and theology

I turn now to the question of what difference a physicalist anthropology might make to theology, given that most Christian theology has in fact been written against the backdrop of one or another dualistic theory. All that physicalist anthropology strictly *requires*, it seems to me, are one or two adjustments: one needs to give up or finesse the doctrine of the intermediate state if that has been an important part of one's tradition. It can be finessed by calling into question the meaningfulness of putting the experiences of those who are with God on an earthly timeline. One needs also to understand resurrection differently: not re-clothing of a "naked" soul with a (new) body, but rather restoring the whole person to life – a new transformed kind of life.

Nonetheless, physicalism does raise interesting questions concerning a variety of theological topics. It is impossible to do justice to all of these here; the following reflections are meant only to be suggestive.

5.1 Doctrine of God

Nicholas Lash, former professor of divinity at Cambridge, notes that a doctrine of God is always correlative to anthropology. For example, when the human person is identified with a solitary mind, God tends to be conceived as a *disembodied* mind, as in the case of classical theism. Much of Lash's own writing argues for the recovery of an embodied and social anthropology in order to recapture a more authentic account of religious experience, but also of a thoroughly trinitarian concept of God.[23]

---

[23] Nicholas Lash, *Easter in Ordinary: Reflections on Human Experience and the Knowledge of God* (Charlottesville, VA: University of Virginia Press, 1986), 95. Cf. Fergus Kerr, *Theology after Wittgenstein*, 2nd edn. (Oxford: SPCK, 1997) for an account of the continuing role of Cartesian anthropology in theology, despite disavowals of Descartes's dualism.

Consider, in contrast, the correlation between certain aspects of Hebraic anthropology and doctrine of God. Aubrey Johnson empha- sizes one important aspect of the Hebraic conception of personhood, which may be contrasted with modern individualism. For moderns, individuals are thought to be "self-contained" in two senses: the first is that they are what they are apart from their relationships. The second is the idea that the real self – the soul or mind or ego – is somehow contained within the body.[24] In contrast, Johnson argues, the Hebraic personality was thought to be extended in subtle ways among the community by means of speech and other forms of communication. This extension of personality is so strong within a household that in its entirety it is regarded as a "psychical whole."[25] "Accordingly, in Israelite thought the individual, as a [nephesh] or centre of power capable of indefinite extension, is never a mere isolated unit ..."[26]

Johnson uses this conception of personhood to elucidate various modes of God's presence. *Ruach*, Spirit, is an extension of Yahweh's personality. Hence God is *genuinely* present in God's messengers (angels), God's word, and God's prophets when they are moved by God's Spirit. "[T]he prophet, in functioning, was held to be more than Yahweh's 'representative'; for the time being he was an active 'Extension' of Yahweh's Personality and, as such, *was* Yahweh 'in Person.'"[27] Johnson rightly points out that this understanding of God's presence is crucial for understanding the later development of trinitarian conceptions of God. I suggest that it is equally important for Christology.

5.2 Christology and Trinity

Early theologians working with a dualist account of humans and an account of Jesus as the pre-existent Son incarnate had problems

---

[24] See sec. 6.1 below.

[25] Aubrey R. Johnson, *The One and the Many in the Israelite Conception of God*, 2nd edn. (Cardiff: University of Wales Press, 1961), 4.

[26] Ibid., 7.   [27] Ibid., 33.

relating all of the "parts." The questions I am asked about Christology when I present a physicalist account of humans often suggest that the questioner is assuming that the divinity of Christ is somehow connected with his soul. Deny the existence of human souls in general and this is tantamount to denying Christ's divinity. However, the assumption lurking behind this question conflicts with the Chalcedonian conclusion that Jesus is both fully divine and fully human.

Given that physicalist anthropology has been widely accepted among theologians for at least a half century, there is a wide array of Christologies developed in this light. I am in no position to do justice to them here.[28] I make here two suggestions. First, rethinking Christology in light of a physicalist anthropology certainly requires Christians to pay adequate attention to incarnation – if humans are purely physical, then there is no getting around the scandal of "en*flesh*ment."

Second, there has always been a tension in trinitarian thought between those who emphasize the unity of God and those who emphasize the three-ness. In the eyes of one group, the others appear to verge on tri-theism; in the eyes of the other, on unitarianism. An alternative approach to the now-popular social trinitarianism emphasizes that the word "person" in formulations of the doctrine of the trinity has shifted its meaning over the centuries. Whereas it now refers to an individual rational agent, the Latin *persona* from which it was derived referred to masks worn by actors and, by extension, to the roles they played. Consequently, Robert Jenson argues that in order to understand the origin of the triune understanding of God, Christians need to "attend to the plot of the biblical narrative turning on these two events [Exodus and Resurrection], and to the *dramatis personae*

---

[28] See, for example, James W. McClendon, Jr.'s "two narratives" Christology, in *Doctrine: Systematic Theology, Volume 2* (Nashville, TN: Abingdon Press, 1994), chapter 6.

who appear in them and carry that plot ..."[29] It is here, he says, that we see how we are led to speak of God as Father, Son, and Spirit. "Thus throughout scripture we encounter *personae* of God's story with his people who are neither simply the same as the story's Lord nor yet other than he. They are precisely *dramatis dei personae*, the personal carriers of a drama that is God's own reality."[30]

With this understanding, we can say that there is one God, Israel's LORD. God at work in the world and in the human community is Spirit; the Hebrew word *ruach* suggests not a substance but an event.[31] God at work (as Spirit) in Jesus is the Messiah, the Incarnate Word, the Son of God.[32] Dunn is one of many who have contributed to the development of "Spirit Christology."[33] This is an approach to Christology that sees the Holy Spirit as the divine aspect of the person of Christ. While Ralph Del Colle argues that Spirit Christology can be reconciled with a three-person account of the trinity,[34] it is clear that it accords much more easily with a oneness trinitarianism, which we might at this point want to call an aspective account in light of Dunn's terminology.

---

[29] Robert W. Jenson, "Trinity," in Adrian Hastings *et al.*, eds., *The Oxford Companion to Christian Thought: Intellectual, Spiritual, and Moral Horizons of Christianity* (Oxford: Oxford University Press, 2000), 715–18.

[30] Ibid. Cf. Aubrey Johnson's account (above) of God's genuine presence in the extensions of his personality, and McClendon's reconciliation of the humanity and divinity of Christ in terms of the intersection of the narrative of human waywardness with the story, beginning in Genesis, of what God has been doing to make a place for his people with himself and thus with one another (*Doctrine*, 275f.).

[31] McClendon, *Doctrine*, 290.

[32] Ibid., 291. Note that Paul sometimes fails to distinguish between the Spirit and the risen Christ; cf. Rom. 8:9–11.

[33] See James D. G. Dunn, *Jesus and the Spirit* (Philadelphia: Westminster, 1975).

[34] Ralph Del Colle, *Christ and the Spirit: Spirit-Christology in Trinitarian Perspective* (Oxford: Oxford University Press, 1994), 4.

5.3 Salvation and history

An equally important doctrine to rethink in light of a physicalist account of human nature is the doctrine of salvation. Again, I can only be suggestive. One of my colleagues recently described some children's literature that uses the device of parallel worlds – worlds just like ours except that one or a few variables are different. For example, what would it be like to be a student at Oxford today if the English Reformation had not taken place? Let us use this device to think about theology in general and the Christian doctrine of salvation in particular. What might theology be like today, and how might Christian history have gone differently, if a physicalist sort of anthropology had predominated rather than dualism? It seems clear that much of the Christian spiritual tradition would be different. There would be no notion of care of the soul as the point of Christian disciplines – certainly no concept of depriving the body in order that the soul might flourish. As some feminist thinkers have been saying for some time: dualist anthropology all too easily leads to disparagement of the body and all that goes along with being embodied. More on Christian spirituality in the next section.

Here are some questions: Without the Neoplatonic notion that the goal of life is to prepare the soul for its proper abode in heaven, would Christians through the centuries have devoted more of their attention to working for God's reign on earth? And would Jesus' teachings be regarded as a proper blueprint for that earthly society? Would the creeds, then, *not* have skipped from his birth to his death, leaving out his teaching and faithful life? Would Christians then see a broader, richer role for Jesus Messiah than as facilitator of the forgiveness of their sins? If Christians had been focusing more, throughout all of these centuries, on following Jesus' teachings about sharing, and about loving our enemies at least enough so as not to kill them, how different might world politics be today? What *would* Christians have been doing these past 2000 years if there were no such things as souls to save?

My reflections here grow out of two sources. One is my own longstanding puzzlement about how the different sorts of Christianity I have encountered can be so different, despite so much doctrinal agreement. For example, the forms of life of my church, the Church of the Brethren, are rather well summed up in the denomination's motto: Continuing the work of Jesus, peacefully, simply, together. Yet at Fuller Seminary, while most of my students are in fact continuing the work of Jesus, their understanding is that Christianity is basically about something else – having one's sins forgiven and eternal life. The second source of my reflections is David Kelsey's book, *The Uses of Scripture in Recent Theology*. He attributes differences among theologies and approaches to scriptural authority to different ideas about how to construe God's presence in the community. He says that a theologian attempts to "catch up what Christianity is basically all about in a single, synoptic, imaginative judgment."[35]

Now, at great risk of oversimplification, I am suggesting that the adoption of a dualist anthropology in the early centuries of the church was largely responsible for changing Christians' conception of what Christianity is basically all about. I am suggesting that original Christianity is better understood in socio-political terms than in terms of what is currently thought of as religious or metaphysical. The adoption of a dualist anthropology provided something different – different from socio-political and ethical concerns – with which Christians became primarily concerned.

This is not, of course, to deny the afterlife. It is rather to emphasize the importance of *bodily* resurrection. It is important to see how the contrasting accounts of life after death – resurrection versus immortality of the soul – lead to different attitudes toward kingdom work in this life. Lutheran theologian Ted Peters whimsically describes the dualist account of salvation as "soul-ectomy." If souls are saved *out of*

---

[35] David Kelsey, *The Uses of Scripture in Recent Theology* (Philadelphia: Westminster, 1975), 159.

this world, then nothing here matters ultimately. If it is our bodily selves that are saved and transformed, then bodies and all that go with them matter – families, history, and all of nature.

Jewish scholar Neil Gillman lends weight to my suggestion. His book, titled *The Death of Death*, argues that resurrection of the body, rather than immortality of the soul, is the only authentically Jewish conception of life after death. Why are physicalism and resurrection important to Jews? For many reasons, Gillman replies:

> Because the notion of immortality tends to deny the reality of death, of God's power to take my life and to restore it; because the doctrine of immortality implies that my body is less precious, important, even "pure," while resurrection affirms that my body is no less God's creation and is both necessary and good; because the notion of a bodiless soul runs counter to my experience of myself and others . . .[36]
>
> It is indispensable for another reason. If my body inserts me into history and society, then the affirmation of bodily resurrection is also an affirmation of history and society. If my bodily existence is insignificant, then so are history and society. To affirm that God has the power to reconstitute me in my bodily existence is to affirm that God also cares deeply about history and society.[37]

Looking forward to the resurrection and transformation of our bodies leads naturally to the expectation that the entire cosmos will be similarly transformed. German theologian Wolfhart Pannenberg argues that in Jesus' resurrection we see the first fruits of the transformation for which the whole creation is longing.[38] As Paul says:

> The created universe is waiting with eager expectation for God's sons to be revealed. It was made subject to frustration, not of its own choice but by the will of him who subjected it, yet with the hope that

---

[36] Gillman, *The Death of Death*, 238.   [37] Ibid., 262.

[38] Wolfhart Pannenberg, *Jesus – God and Man* (Philadelphia, PA: Westminster Press, 1968).

29

the universe itself is to be freed from the shackles of mortality and is to enter upon the glorious liberty of the children of God. Up to the present, as we know, the whole created universe in all its parts groans as if in the pangs of childbirth. What is more, we also, to whom the Spirit is given as the first fruits of the harvest to come, are groaning inwardly while we look forward to our adoption, our liberation from mortality. (Rom. 8:19–23 [REB])

6. Questioning the spiritual quest

In the previous section I have only begun to scratch the surface of important theological issues related to one's theory of human nature. The change from a dualist to a physicalist anthropology also calls for serious reconsideration of traditional understandings of Christian spirituality. From Augustine to the present we have had a conception of the self that distinguishes the inner life from the outer, and spirituality has been associated largely with the inner.[39]

6.1 Augustinian inwardness

The distinction between inner and outer is not equivalent to the distinction between soul and body, but its historical origin was a result of Augustine's dualism. The peculiar notion that one has an "inside," and that one's true self can "enter into" that inner space, arose from Augustine's reflections on the problem of the location of the soul. He came to conceive of it as a "space" of its own. The ancient rhetorical tradition, with its arts of memory and invention, had already connected the idea of chambers or rooms with the idea of memory. Orators memorized the order of subjects to be discussed

---

[39] See Phillip Cary, *Augustine's Invention of the Inner Self: The Legacy of a Christian Platonist* (Oxford: Oxford University Press, 2000).

in a speech by imagining themselves walking through the rooms of a familiar house and mentally marking each successive place with an image that would serve as a reminder of the next topic. The result was the introduction, in Augustine's *Confessions*, of the idea of memory as a capacious inner chamber, in which is found "innumerable images of all kinds ... whatever we think about ... all the skills acquired through the liberal arts ... the principles of the laws of numbers ..." and most important of all, God.[40]

The combination of the Neoplatonic emphasis on the care of the soul with Augustine's metaphor of entering into one's own self or soul in order to find God constituted a complex of ideas that has shaped the whole of Western spirituality from that point onward. Teresa of Avila's extended metaphor of the interior castle is one of its finest fruits.[41] Teresa writes:

> ... we consider our soul to be like a castle made entirely out of a diamond or of very clear crystal, in which there are many rooms, just as in heaven there are many dwelling places ... [T]he soul of the just person is nothing else but a paradise where the Lord says He finds His delight. I didn't find anything comparable to the magnificent beauty of a soul and its marvelous capacity. Indeed, our intellects, however keen, can hardly comprehend it, just as they cannot comprehend God; but He Himself says that He created us in His own image and Likeness ...
>
> Well, let us consider that this castle has, as I said, many dwelling places: some up above, others down below, others to the sides; and in the center and middle is the main dwelling place where the very secret exchanges between God and the soul take place.[42]

---

[40] Augustine, *Confessions*, Book 10; trans. Henry Chadwick (Oxford. Oxford University Press, 1991), 185.

[41] Teresa of Avila, *The Interior Castle*, written in 1577.

[42] Teresa, *Interior Castle*, in *The Collected Works of St. Teresa of Avila*, vol. 2, trans. and ed. Otilio Rodriguez and Kieran Kavanaugh (Washington, DC: Institute of Carmelite Studies, 1980), 283–4.

This imagery is so familiar to us that we often fail to notice how strange it is: I, the *real* I, am somehow *inside* of *myself*. Teresa does note the oddity: "Well, getting back to our beautiful and delightful castle we must see how we can enter it. It seems I'm saying something foolish. For if this castle is the soul, clearly one doesn't have to enter it since it is within oneself."[43]

6.2 Contemporary revisions

There are a number of thoughtful critics today of this tradition of inwardness. One is Nicholas Lash;[44] another is Owen Thomas, emeritus professor of theology at the Episcopal Divinity School. I shall follow two of Thomas's essays.[45] Here are the contemporary misunderstandings as Thomas sees them:

> It is commonly assumed that spirituality is an optional matter, that some people are more spiritual than others and some not at all, that spirituality is essentially a good thing (the more the better), that while spirituality is somehow related to religion it should be sharply distinguished from religion as something superior to and more important than religion . . .[46]

Thomas argues his position on the basis of the very narrow meaning of the word "spirit" in English as compared with its translations in other languages – *Geist* in German, *esprit* in French, and *spirito* in Italian. The English word "spirit" is associated with emotion and will as opposed to intellect. In contrast, the German *Geist* refers to the totality of what defines humanity in its fullness. Consequently, Thomas believes that spirituality "is most fruitfully defined as the sum of all the uniquely human capacities

---

[43] Ibid., 285. [44] Lash, *Easter in Ordinary*.

[45] Owen Thomas, "Some Problems in Contemporary Christian Theology," *Anglican Theological Review* 82, no. 2 (Spring 2000): 267–81, and essay cited at note 52.

[46] Ibid., 267.

and functions: self-awareness, self-transcendence, memory, antici-pation, rationality (in its broadest sense), creativity, plus the moral, intellectual, social, political, aesthetic, and religious capacities, all understood as embodied."[47] If this is the case, then all humans are spiritual to some degree, and spirituality can be either good or bad.

This conception of spirituality cuts against the tendency to associate spirituality with the inner and religion with the outer life of institutions, practices, doctrines, and moral codes. The tradi-tional notion of spirituality has assumed that the inner encounter with God is the *source* of the external forms of religious observance. However, a variety of philosophers and theologians have questioned this assumption. Instead we need to recognize the ways in which language (which is necessarily public) and other social practices provide the individual with the resources for private, inner experi-ence. To put it quite simply, the lone individual might indeed have an experience of God, but without any theological language would have no way of *knowing* what the experience was. The more linguis-tic resources and expectations provided by one's tradition the more nuanced one's experiences will be.

Thomas cites George Lindbeck's work on the cultural–linguistic formation of religious sensibilities,[48] Fergus Kerr's Wittgensteinian critique of the theology of inwardness as essentially gnostic,[49] and Alasdair MacIntyre's critique of the privatization of morality.[50]

Thomas's embodied and wide-ranging account of spirituality is in sharp contrast to what a variety of commentators see as the predominant religious sensibilities of Americans. Literary critic Harold Bloom says that "the real American religion is and always has been in fact ... gnosticism." "It is a knowing, by and of an

---

[47] Ibid., 268.

[48] George A. Lindbeck, *The Nature of Doctrine: Religion and Theology in a Postliberal Age* (Philadelphia: Westminster, 1984).

[49] Kerr, *Theology after Wittgenstein*.

[50] Alasdair MacIntyre, *After Virtue: A Study in Moral Theory*, 2nd edn. (Notre Dame: University of Notre Dame Press, 1984).

uncreated self, of self-within-the-world, and the knowledge leads to freedom ... from nature, time, history, community, and other selves ..."[51]

It is one of the great paradoxes of Christian history, Thomas notes, that on the one hand the biblical tradition seems to emphasize the primacy of the outer – the body, speech, action – while on the other hand, the Christian spiritual tradition from Augustine to today has emphasized the inner. It was not that the biblical authors did not know of the inner/outer distinction. In particular, Jesus' teaching distinguished the *heart* as the source of intellectual, emotional, and volitional energies from outward behavior.[52] Yet, in general,

> from the call of Abraham and Moses to the Decalogue of the Sinai covenant, the covenants with David, the preaching of the eighth-century prophets, and Jesus' teaching about the reign of God, the biblical emphasis is on the outer: faith manifest and visible in obedience, sacrifice, and just action; repentance shown in the rending of garments and weeping; thanksgiving seen in dancing, singing, and feasting, and the reign of God perceived in preaching and healing and compared to buying a pearl, sowing seed, and holding a feast.[53]

Thomas's prescription for restoring proper balance between inner and outer is as follows: within this reformulation there must be, first, a renewed emphasis in Christian formation on the significance of the body, the material, social, economic, political, and historical world rather than an exclusive focus on the soul or interior life. This emphasis is obviously founded on the centrality in Christian faith of the themes of creation, incarnation, history, and

---

[51] Harold Bloom, *The American Religion: The Emergence of the Post-Christian Nation* (New York: Simon and Schuster, 1992), 49.

[52] Owen C. Thomas, "Interiority and Christian Spirituality," *Journal of Religion* 80, 1 (2000): 41–60.

[53] Ibid., 52.

consummation, including the resurrection of the body. Although there has been considerable attention devoted to the body in recent Christian spirituality, it has been largely focused on using the body as a foil for the progress of the soul.

Second, the reign of God must become central again in Christian spirituality. The reign of God is the fundamental theme of Jesus' mission: its inbreaking and manifestation in Jesus' presence, healing, and teaching. To be a follower of Jesus means to repent and open oneself to the presence of this reign, to look for and point to signs of the reign, and to participate in it by manifesting its signs in active love of the neighbor and in the struggle for justice and peace. The presence of the reign of God is manifest primarily in outer life and public life, as well as in inner life and private life, and it is the former which has been largely ignored in recent Christian formation.[54]

Earlier in this section I pointed out that the inner–outer distinction is not the same as the distinction between soul and body. So presumably one could be a body–soul dualist while avoiding an excessively inward-looking spirituality. In fact, some of the greatest writers on inwardness did so. Teresa of Avila spent years traveling, reforming convents, and founding new ones. It is also possible for someone with a physicalist anthropology to flee from the responsibilities of kingdom work by turning to solitude, self-examination, and contemplation. So the strongest point I can make here is to claim, as I did in the preceding section, that physicalism – along with an eschatological hope for resurrection of the body – leads more *naturally* to a concern for the physical world and its transformation than does dualism.

I need to raise an important issue here, but one I shall reserve for the next chapter. This is the problem of divine action. In the distant past, Christians believed that God had to do with both souls and bodies. However, during the modern period, it became difficult to

---

[54] Thomas, "Some Problems," 278.

give an account of how God could act in the physical world without running foul of the laws of nature. One strategy was to say that God works only in human history, not in nature. But if we humans conceive of ourselves as purely physical, this strategy is no longer available. The difficult question of how God acts in the physical world cannot be avoided. James McClendon says that we have so anthropocentrized our theology in the modern period that we have a difficult time appreciating the fact that God has to do with *bodies*. He follows William Temple in describing Christianity as "the most avowedly materialist of all the great religions."[55] Although we can never describe what Austin Farrer calls the "causal joint" between God and matter,[56] we have to accept the fact that God does indeed act in the physical world, and in particular, however awkward it may sound, we have to say that God acts causally on human brains.[57]

7. Retrospect

I began this chapter by noting that Christians and others in our culture subscribe to a surprising variety of theories of human nature. The odd thing is that we are generally unaware of these differences. I hazard a guess that some of you readers may not even know what your spouse thinks about this issue. Unbeknownst to you, you may be sleeping with a trichotomist!

I have begun in this chapter to make a cumulative case for physicalism. I want to make three summary points: first, most of

[55] See James W. McClendon, Jr., *Ethics: Systematic Theology, Volume 1*, revised edn. (Nashville: Abingdon, 2002), 97; referring to William Temple, *Nature, Man and God* (London: Macmillan, 1934), 478. However, this seems equally true of Judaism.

[56] Austin Farrer, *Faith and Speculation* (London, A. & C. Black, 1967), 66.

[57] See Robert J. Russell, Nancey Murphy, Theo C. Meyering, and Michael A. Arbib, eds., *Neuroscience and the Person: Scientific Perspectives on Divine Action* (Vatican City State and Berkeley, CA: Vatican Observatory and Center for Theology and the Natural Sciences, 1999).

the dualism that has *appeared* to be biblical teaching has been a result of poor translations. The original Aramaic and Hebrew terms were first translated into Greek, and later taken to mean what Greek philosophers would mean by them. These meanings come down to us in older English translations. After the translations have been fixed, it is hard to find any clear *teaching* on the metaphysical make-up of the person – this is simply not a question in which the biblical authors were interested. They apparently assumed a variety of extant views and then used and remodeled them for their own purposes. So insofar as the Bible is normative for Christians, it appears that contemporary Christians are free to adopt either physicalism or dualism.

Second, despite lack of clarity on this issue in the Bible, it is in fact the case that most Christians, throughout most of their history, have been dualists of one sort or another. However, the fact that this has been largely due to cultural influences should free contemporary Christians to formulate accounts of human nature that are in keeping with *current* cultural developments. In the following chapter I shall survey some of the scientific developments that have long called dualism into question.

Third, I have argued that the adoption of a physicalist anthropology might lead to a reformulation of theology, both systematic theology and the theology of spirituality, that would correct for the otherworldliness and excessive inwardness of the Platonists, and that this might be a good thing both for our relationship with God and for our relations with the Earth and the rest of her inhabitants.

2 | What does science say about human nature? Physics, evolutionary biology, and neuroscience

1. Prospect

In chapter 1, I noted the fact that we have a wide variety of views of human nature available to us in our culture: trichotomism, dualism, physicalism, idealism and many variations on each of these themes. I claimed that the variety can be explained in part by the fact that Christian theologians have taught a number of different views throughout the tradition's long history. Many of these differences are due to the borrowing of assorted accounts from ancient philosophy. Other differences are due to conflicting interpretations of the biblical texts. I made a claim there, which might not be so widely accepted as these others, that there is no such thing as *the* biblical view of human nature. I argued that the scriptural authors were interested in the various dimensions of human life, in relationships, not in the philosophical question of how many parts are essential components of a human being. This virtual silence in Scripture has made it easy for Christians throughout their history to adopt and adapt a variety of cultural assumptions about human nature.

I also claimed that there were only three major points in church history when Christians were forced to re-evaluate their theories of human nature. One in the early centuries was occasioned by the spread of Christianity into more Hellenized regions of the Mediterranean world. The second was the Aristotelian revival in the late middle ages, occasioned by Muslim conquests in Europe. The third was the development in the modern period of historical-critical methodology.

My plan in this chapter is to turn to scientific influences. I shall argue that there are three major points in Western history where *science* has called for a re-appraisal of theories of human nature. The first was the replacement of Aristotelian physics by modern physics in the seventeenth century. This called for a different account of the nature of the soul, and occasioned a return to a more radical dualism. A consequence of the changes in conceptions of both matter and the soul was creation of what is now judged to be an insuperable problem by most philosophers: the means by which body and soul (or mind) interact.

The second major scientific change was the Darwinian revolution in biology. This has had wide-ranging effects on human self-understanding, but relates to the dualism/physicalism debate in that it raised, for some, the question of why humans should be thought to have souls if their close animal kin do not. Others responded with an emphasis on dualism as the very thing that distinguishes us from animals. This issue of human distinctiveness will occupy us in chapter 4 as well.

The third major scientific impact is taking place right now due to the influences of contemporary neuroscience. It is becoming increasingly obvious to many that the functions and attributes once attributed to the soul or mind are better understood as functions of the brain. We shall examine each of these developments in turn. Despite the fact that the evolutionary theories of Charles Darwin (1809–82) have been seen by so many as a challenge to Christian faith, I believe that the developments in physics and in the neurosciences have both been as much *or more* significant in reshaping theories of human nature.

2. The atomist revolution in physics

Galileo and Copernicus are famous for their roles in promoting heliocentric astronomy. This revolution is said to have had a great impact on human self-understanding in that it displaced us from the center of the universe. However, there were further, and I would say, much more important repercussions. Displacement of the Earth from the center of the universe spelled the end of physics based on Aristotle's hylomorphic conception of matter, and soon resulted in the development of corpuscular or atomist theories in physics, which in turn called for a radically new conception of the human person.

2.1 The medieval world-picture

In my first chapter I mentioned that Thomas Aquinas, in the thirteenth century, adopted Aristotle's theory of matter. This theory continued to provide the basis for physics until the seventeenth century. The difference between atomism and hylomorphism depends on how one answers this question: Is matter infinitely divisible? Ancient atomism was based on the assumption that matter is *not* infinitely divisible; at some point one comes to particles that are "uncuttable." The word "atom" means, literally, uncuttable. Democritus and the other ancient atomists believed that the differences between one kind of material substance and another could be explained in terms of the qualities and organization of the atoms of which they are composed.

If one is *not* an atomist, then one needs an alternative account of the differences among material substances – what makes butter different from stone? Aristotle's answer was inspired by Plato's concept of the *forms* or *ideas*. Plato's forms existed eternally in a transcendent realm and served as something like blueprints for material entities. In contrast, Aristotle believed that they were inherent in the material beings that they *formed*. It is the form that gives a thing its operative powers and directs its development. Transmission of the form in reproduction is what ensures that living things produce their own kinds. The forms of living things are also called souls. Plants, animals, and humans, according to both

Aristotle and Thomas, have nutritive, sensitive, and rational souls, respectively.

Aristotle understood all motion on the model of biological change: because of their forms, things have their own particular essences that endow them with goal-directedness – for example, the acorn is endowed with the drive or tendency to grow into an oak tree. This thesis, combined with the ancient theory of the four elements – earth, water, air, and fire – provided an account of "natural" motions. At the same time it tied Aristotelian physics to astronomy. The natural place of the element earth is the Earth – the center of the universe. Water, air, and fire naturally form concentric spheres around the Earth. Material things are composed of greater or lesser proportions of the element earth and therefore have a greater or lesser tendency to move toward the surface of the Earth when they are not constrained. They seek their natural positions.

Thomas and his contemporaries in the late middle ages resolved contradictions between Aristotle's thought and the Christian tradition, and in so doing produced a worldview that we might call a cosmo-theology. Historian of science Thomas Kuhn notes, however, that the very detail and erudition of these works made the new synthesis inaccessible to most. It was by means of the poetry of Dante that the new worldview came to grip the Christian imagination.[1]

Dante's *Divine Comedy* is a description of the poet's journey through the universe as conceived by the fourteenth-century Christian. The poet descends from the surface of the Earth to the nine circles of Hell, which mirror the nine celestial spheres above. From the vilest region, the center of the universe housing the Devil and his minions, he returns to the surface at the other side and encounters the mount of purgatory, which allows him to ascend through the spheres of air and fire to the celestial spheres and finally

---

[1] Thomas S. Kuhn, *The Copernican Revolution: Planetary Astronomy in the Development of Western Thought* (Cambridge, MA: Harvard University Press, 1957), 112.

encounter the throne of God. Kuhn's account of the theological significance of this world picture is worth quoting at length:

> For the Christian . . . the new universe had symbolic as well as literal meaning, and it was this Christian symbolism that Dante wished most of all to display. Through allegory his *Divine Comedy* made it appear that the medieval universe could have had no other structure than the Aristotelian–Ptolemaic. As he portrays it, the universe of spheres mirrors both man's hope and his fate. Both physically and spiritually man occupies a crucial intermediate position in this universe filled, as it is, by a hierarchical chain of substances that stretches from the inert clay of the center to the pure spirit of the Empyrean. Man is compounded of a material body and a spiritual soul: all other substances are either matter or spirit. Man's location, too, is intermediate: the earth's surface is close to its debased and corporeal center but within sight of the celestial periphery which surrounds it symmetrically. Man lives in squalor and uncertainty, and he is very close to Hell. But his central location is strategic, for he is everywhere under the eye of God. Both man's double nature and his intermediate position enforce the choice from which the drama of Christianity is compounded. He may follow his corporeal, earthly nature down to its natural place at the corrupt center, or he may follow his soul upward through the successively more spiritual spheres until he reaches God. As one critic of Dante has put it, in the Divine Comedy the "vastest of all themes, the theme of human sin and salvation, is adjusted to the great plan of the universe."[2] Once this adjustment had been achieved, any change in the plan of the universe would inevitably affect the drama of Christian life and Christian death. To move the earth was to break the continuous chain of created being.[3]

---

[2] Kuhn refers here to Charles H. Grandgent, *Discourses on Dante* (Cambridge, MA: Harvard University Press, 1924), 93.

[3] Kuhn, op. cit, 112–13.

2.2 The Copernican challenge

The challenge to the Christian worldview represented by the displacement of humankind from this "strategic location" is well known. Our emphasis here is on the consequences of the Copernican revolution for understanding the "microcosm" – the human being itself.

If Copernicus's heliocentric theory is accepted, there is no longer an explanation in Aristotelian terms of why heavy objects fall toward the surface of the Earth. A whole new physics was required, and the obvious move was to attempt to resuscitate ancient atomism. So by early in the seventeenth century the Copernicans were ranged against the scholastic philosophers, attempting to explain motion, both earthly and heavenly, in atomist terms.

Atomism, of course, was wildly successful in physics. Our interest is in the consequences of this change for theories of human nature. The most direct effect was that the soul could no longer be understood as the form of the body; in this new worldview there simply is no such thing as a form.[4] There were two obvious responses. One was physicalism, first embraced by Thomas Hobbes (1588–1697). Hobbes's entire account of human nature was based on the notion of particles in motion. Sensation is due to pressure on the sense organs; thinking is a matter of small motions in the head; and emotions are due to motions about the heart. Hobbes is best known now for his political philosophy. He sought to understand the commonwealth in terms of the attractive and repulsive forces among atomistic individuals. Hobbes's physicalism did not have a great deal of influence, but the individualism he espoused continues to be influential to this day.

---

[4] However, see Eleonore Stump, "Non-Cartesian Substance Dualism and Materialism without Reductionism," *Faith and Philosophy* 12, no. 4 (October 1995): 505–31. Stump argues that form for Thomas is best understood as a "configurational state," and that current biology bears out the thesis that biological entities need to be understood in terms of both matter and configuration.

René Descartes (1596–1650) chose the other obvious option in response to the demise of the Aristotelian account of the person. He chose to return to a radical dualism of mind (or soul) and body along the lines of Plato's and Augustine's theories. Descartes distinguished two basic kinds of created realities, extended substance (*res extensa* in Latin) and thinking substance (*res cogitans*); the latter included angels and human minds. It is difficult to overemphasize the importance of this radical distinction between the material and the non-material for later thought.

Notice that there is a linguistic shift here from "souls" to "minds." Either term is a fair translation of Descartes's Latin or French. For Thomas the mind was equivalent to the rational soul (intellect and will). For Descartes, everything of which we are conscious, including sensations, is a function of the mind,[5] and all of the other faculties (such as the ability to move) are attributed to the body. Earlier translations of Descartes's writings used "soul," but as this term has increasingly taken on religious connotations, translators have come to prefer the word "mind" in most contexts. In contrast to the Aristotelians, Descartes believed that only humans have souls. Animals and the human body are complex hydraulic machines.

The shift from hylomorphism to atomism and substance dualism created what is now seen by many to be an insoluble problem: mind–body interaction. Whereas for Aristotle and his followers the soul was but one instance of form, in modern thought the mind becomes an anomaly in an otherwise purely material world of nature. Furthermore, *the very conception of matter has changed.* Before the atomist revolution, matter and form had been correlative concepts – matter was that which had the potential to be activated by form. Matter (at least as unformed, prime matter) was entirely passive. For early modern thinkers, matter is also passive, inert. But

---

[5] See Richard Rorty, *Philosophy and the Mirror of Nature* (Princeton, NJ: Princeton University Press, 1979) for reflections on the peculiarity of counting all of such disparate experiences as "mental."

now, instead of being moved by immanent forms, it is moved by external forces – physical forces. This creates a dilemma: hold on to the immateriality of mind, and there is no way to account for its supposed ability to move the body; interpret it as a quasi-physical force and its effects ought to be measurable and quantifiable as is any other force in nature. But nothing of the latter enters into modern physics.

Lest one conclude that the problems of mind–body interaction are merely the result of too crude a view of physical interactions in early modern physics, it is important to note that contemporary physics presents comparable complications. Now the problem has to do with the law of conservation of matter and energy: if Descartes is right that a nonphysical mind can cause the body to move, then there must be a transfer of energy to the body. In order for physical energy to be transferred to any physical system, it has to have been transferred from some other physical system. Philosopher Owen Flanagan asks how, for example, the mind's decision to go to a concert results in the body getting up and going:

> But the mind, according to Descartes, is not a physical system and therefore it does not have any energy to transfer. The mind cannot account for the fact that our body ends up at the concert.
>
> If we accept the principle of the conservation of energy we seem committed either to denying that the nonphysical mind exists, or to denying that it could cause anything to happen, or to making some very implausible ad hoc adjustments in our physics. For example, we could maintain that the principle of conservation of energy holds, but that every time a mind introduces new energy into the world – thanks to some mysterious capacity it has – an equal amount of energy departs from the physical universe – thanks to some perfectly orchestrated mysterious capacity the universe has.[6]

[6] Owen Flanagan, *The Science of the Mind*, 2nd edn., (Cambridge, MA: MIT Press, 1991), 21.

It is worth mentioning the epistemological problems created by this metaphysical shift. For Aristotelians, sensory knowledge resulted from the transference of the form of the thing perceived into the intellect of the perceiver, whose mind was, literally, in-*formed* by exactly that which makes the object to be what it is. Thus, exact knowledge of the essences of things was possible on the basis of very little observation. Perceptual *error* is what needed explanation.

In a world composed of atoms, sensation must result from the impinging of atoms on the sensory membranes, and then from coded information conveyed to the brain and thence to the mind. Ideas in the mind are no longer identical to the forms inherent in things, but mere representations produced by a complicated process of transmission, encoding, and decoding. Thus arises modern skepticism with regard to sense perception.[7]

Descartes's solution was to begin with the Augustinian notion that we know our own souls/minds directly.[8] But for early modern philosophers that is *all* we know directly. As Nicholas Lash points out, on this account, the problems of knowledge are presented as if they were problems of engineering – how to make contact, build bridges, with what is "outside."[9] Descartes reassured himself of the possibility of (indirect) knowledge of the external world by arguing that a benevolent creator would not have constructed us so as to be constantly deceived. Contemporary philosophy is still struggling with these issues.

---

[7] See Theo C. Meyering, *Historical Roots of Cognitive Science: The Rise of a Cognitive Theory of Perception from Antiquity to the Nineteenth Century* (Dordrecht: Kluwer Academic Publishers, 1989).

[8] Owen Flanagan uses results from current neuroscience to call into question this philosophical assumption concerning the priority of self-knowledge. See *The Science of the Mind*, 194–200.

[9] Nicholas Lash, *Easter in Ordinary: Reflections on Human Experience and the Knowledge of God* (Charlottesville, VA: University Press of Virginia, 1986), 69.

3. The Darwinian revolution

The Darwinian theory of evolution has had an impact on contemporary culture comparable to that of the revolution in physics and astronomy that heralded the beginning of modern science. One of many issues it raised was that of continuity between humans and (other) animals. One way to interpret this continuity was to take it as an additional reason to question any form of body–soul or body–mind dualism. Recall that Descartes described animals in purely material, and, in fact, mechanical terms. Given the rejection of the scholastic idea of animal souls, the recognition of human kinship with and development from lower animals warranted the conclusion, in the eyes of many, that humans, too, are purely material.

Many Christians evaded this materialist conclusion by granting that the human body is a product of biological evolution, but maintaining that God creates a soul for each individual at conception. This intellectual maneuver was adopted by many Evangelical Protestants and also by Pope Pius XII. It runs into difficulties, however, when we ask when the *human* species appeared. Contemporary biologists now offer a very complex account of human origins in which there is no clear distinction between animals and humans. The branch of the evolutionary tree leading from our common ancestors with the apes to modern humans began five to seven million years ago and includes at least three predecessor hominid species, as well as some other hominids not in the direct line of descent to modern humans.[10] Were our first hominid ancestors human, or are only modern humans truly human, or did the change take place somewhere in between? What about hominid

[10] Francisco J. Ayala, "Human Nature: One Evolutionist's View," in Warren Brown, Nancey Murphy, and H. Newton Malony, eds., *Whatever Happened to the Soul? Scientific and Theological Portraits of Human Nature* (Minneapolis: Fortress Press, 1998), 31–48.

species such as the Neanderthals that are not in the direct line of descent to modern humans? To claim that humans alone have the gift of a soul seems to force an arbitrary distinction where there is much evidence for continuity.

If human distinctiveness cannot be attributed to the unique possession of a soul or immaterial mind, in what *does* it consist? This has become an intriguing philosophical and theological issue – one likely to benefit from continuing scientific investigation of actual similarities and differences between ourselves and the other higher primates. We shall pursue the issue of human distinctiveness in chapter 4.

Development of the science of genetics has contributed to the discussion of human nature initiated by the theory of evolution. The biochemical explanation of heredity solidified the evolutionary account of human origins. It also contributed new evidence for human continuity with the other species: all other life forms possess DNA, and there may not be *any* genes unique to the human species.[11] In genetic terms we are more closely related to chimpanzees than the chimpanzees are to the other great apes!

3.1 Our embarrassing relatives

Holding to a dualist account of humans appears to solve the "problem" of distinguishing us from animals. *But why is continuity with animals seen as a problem in the first place?* I have two theories. One is based on the idea famously described by Arthur Lovejoy as "the great chain of being."[12] This is a Hellenistic idea that shaped Western consciousness from the days of classical Greece through the end of the middle ages. The quotation from Kuhn above

---

[11] See V. Elving Anderson, "A Genetic View of Human Nature," in Brown *et al.*, eds., *Whatever Happened to the Soul?*, 49–72; 50.

[12] Arthur O. Lovejoy, *The Great Chain of Being* (Cambridge, MA: Harvard University Press, 1936).

describes the late medieval version. Everything that exists, from rocks to God, can be arranged in a hierarchy: inorganic materials, plants, animals, humans, angels, and God. The great ontological divide here is not between Creator and creatures, as I think it should be for readers of the Bible, but rather between matter and spirit ("spirit" understood in gnostic rather than Pauline terms). Humans on this view are "amphibious" creatures, their bodies are on the lower side of the great divide, their souls above. This being a hierarchy of value and not merely a classificatory scheme, Westerners have grown accustomed to thinking of themselves as distinctly superior to animals in moral terms. I believe that this is one of the sources of negative attitudes toward animals. They are "beastly," while we are (when we behave in ways commensurate with our place in the hierarchy) "humane."[13]

The holdover from this very old worldview, I believe, is part of the explanation for resistance to accepting the fact of our close kinship with animals. Another explanation is connected with Darwin's theory itself, but ultimately comes from the natural *theology* of Darwin's day. Contemporary ethologist Frans de Waal has written extensively on the behavior of social animals. An important aim of his work is to counteract a scientific culture that is ready to describe animal behavior in morally negative terms – for example, some chimpanzees are called "cheaters" or "grudgers," and kinship bonds are called "nepotism." Yet these same scientists refuse to use any language with a positive moral tone. De Waal shows that human capacities for morality, such as sharing food and caring for the sick or disabled, have quite striking predecessors among certain species of animals. Here is one of the instances he presents as evidence:

> A British ethologist . . . followed the final days of a low ranking adult male [in a dwarf mongoose colony; it was] dying of chronic kidney

---

[13] See Mary Midgley, *Beast and Man: The Roots of Human Nature* (Ithaca, NY: Cornell University Press, 1978).

disease. The male lived in a captive group consisting of a pair and its offspring. Two adjustments took place. First, the sick male was allowed to eat much earlier in the rank order than previously ... Second, the rest of the group changed from sleeping on elevated objects, such as boxes, to sleeping on the floor once the sick male had lost the ability to climb up onto the boxes. They stayed in contact with him, grooming him much more than usual. After the male's death, the group slept with the cadaver until its decay made removal necessary.[14]

So here is the question again: why the preference for viewing animals in a negative moral light. De Waal suggests (in a section titled "Calvinist Sociobiology") that the source is Christian conceptions of the Fall according to which all of nature is corrupted.[15] I argue, though, that a more proximate cause is the moral and theological climate in which Darwin worked.

3.2 Theological roots of social Darwinism

The common assumption is that Darwin began with observations of nature, then formulated a theory about the fierce struggle for existence among animals, and then, after that, moral theories called social Darwinism were formulated. The reasoning went as follows: what is natural among animals – struggle and strife – is good because it leads to evolutionary progress. Therefore what is natural for us human animals must be competition and strife, and that, too, will lead to progress, only here it is economic rather than biological progress.

What this story leaves out is the fact that Darwin was predisposed by the *theology* of his day to see nature in overwhelmingly conflictual terms. Darwin was influenced by William Paley and his design

[14] Frans de Wall, *Good Natured: The Origins of Right and Wrong in Humans and Other Animals* (Cambridge, MA: Harvard University Press, 1996), 80.
[15] Ibid., 13–20.

argument.[16] Paley's work conditioned Darwin and his followers to see features of nature as specifically and intentionally designed by God. So Darwin was predisposed to read off the character, the intentions, and the activities of God from the characteristics of the natural world.

A second ingredient in Darwin's thinking is found in the work of Thomas Malthus, in his *Essay on the Principle of Population* (1798). The principle of population states that population, if unchecked, will grow geometrically, whereas food supply will increase, at most, arithmetically. Struggle, competition, and starvation are the natural result. Malthus's principle of population was the key to Darwin's thinking. It had already been proposed that one species could change into another; already the great age of the earth had been established by the geologists. So what was missing was the *mechanism* to get from one species to another.

From the study of domesticated animals Darwin came to the conclusion that selection was the principle of change. Then, reading Malthus, he saw how to extend this principle to the natural world: animals breed without "the moral restraint which in some small degree checks the increase in mankind."[17] Therefore, "the pressure is always ready ... A thousand wedges are being forced into the economy of nature ... The final cause of all this wedging must be to sort out proper structure and adapt it to change."[18] So Darwin concluded that it is the competition for food that produces the mechanism of change.

It is important to note that Malthus was an Anglican clergyman, who was working in the tradition of eighteenth-century natural theology. So his book was not simply a scientific treatise on population growth and food supply, but rather it was a *theodicy* – an

---

[16] William Paley, *Natural Theology* (1802).

[17] Darwin, quoted in Robert M. Young, *Darwin's Metaphor: Nature's Place in Victorian Culture* (Cambridge: Cambridge University Press, 1985), 41.

[18] Darwin's notes, quoted in Young, op. cit., 41f.

attempt to reconcile the goodness of God with evil and suffering. In place of Paley's "myriads of happy beings" Malthus sees struggle, inequality, suffering, and death as the basic features of the natural world. And these are interpreted by him as the result of divine providence. So Paley had set everyone up to believe that, whatever the character of the natural order, that is the way God designed it. Malthus's role was to say that the character of the natural world is competition and starvation. This, then, reflects on God's intentions and it is also seen as providential. Malthus wrote that evil produces exertion, exertion produces mind, and mind produces progress. So in the end it is *providential* that there is *not* enough food to go around.

The difference between eighteenth-century political and economic views and those after Malthus was a loss of optimism. The limits placed on economic growth by the limits on food production meant that the growing population of urban poor was seen in terms of surplus mouths rather than as an economically beneficial surplus of labor. In response, Malthus and his followers argued that relief to the poor should be restricted since it only postponed the collapse of those who could not support themselves. Malthus argued that a law should be passed such that no child born from any marriage more than a year after the law was passed should be entitled to parish assistance.[19] After Malthus it was not uncommon for other theologians to take up the cause. Thomas Chalmers, professor of divinity at the University of Edinburgh, emphasized the necessity of moral restraint, especially sexual restraint, if the poor were to avoid the miseries to which the principle of population would lead. The necessary connection between moral weakness and misery was a reflection of the very character of God. Chalmers wrote:

> It is not the lesson of conscience, that God would, under the mere impulse of parental fondness for the creatures whom He has made,

---

[19] Young, op. cit., 38.

let down the high state and sovereignty which belong to Him; or that He would forebear the infliction of the penalty, because of any soft or timid shrinking from the pain it would give the objects of His displeasure ... [W]hen one looks to the disease and the agony of spirit, and above all the hideous and unsparing death, with its painful struggles and gloomy forebodings, which are spread universally over the face of the earth – we cannot ... imagine of the God who presides over such an economy, that He is ... a being who will falter from the imposition of his severity, which might serve the objects of a high administration.[20]

So, a rather gloomy view of God and God's purposes! The question then is what role Darwinian theory played in the development of "social Darwinism." Historian Robert Young says that all Darwin's theory actually did was to provide a simple change in the source of the justification for social stratification. Now the basis of social stratification among rich and poor

> ... changes from a theological theodicy to a biological one in which the so-called physiological division of labor provides a scientific guarantee of the rightness of the property and work relations of industrial society ...
>
> The famous controversy in the nineteenth century between science and theology was very heated indeed, and scholars have concentrated on this level of analysis. However, at another level, the protagonists in the debate were in fundamental agreement. They were fighting over the best ways of rationalizing the same set of assumptions about the existing order. An explicitly theological theodicy was being challenged by a secular one based on biological conceptions and the fundamental assumption of the uniformity of nature.[21]

---

[20] Thomas Chalmers, *The Adaptation of External Nature to the Moral and Intellectual Constitution of Man*, 2 vols., Bridgewater Treatises (London: Pickering, 1833), 292f.

[21] Young, *Darwin's Metaphor*, 191.

So the theological context in which Darwin's theory was developed was largely responsible for the conflictual imagery in Darwin's language. It is not surprising, therefore, that his theory could be used to support the same social agenda as that which contributed to its development. Now this raises another question. If Darwin's theory of how nature works was influenced by thinkers such as Malthus and Chalmers, has this affected *only* his theory of natural selection, or has it affected his and subsequent scientists' *perceptions* of nature itself? The recent work of de Waal and others confirms that this is true.

In short, I am suggesting several possible sources of moral objections to recognizing our kinship with the rest of the animal world, but close scrutiny shows these to be insubstantial. The relevance of this to my central argument, of course, is to question in yet another manner the need for a dualist anthropology. We do *not* need to think of ourselves as having souls in order to distance ourselves from the rest of God's mammalian creatures. In fact, recognition of our humble origins is deeply biblical.[22]

In chapter 3 I shall return to the issue of human distinctiveness.

4. Neuroscience and the soul

So far I have argued (in section 2) that the development of modern physics created an apparently insoluble problem for dualism, the problem of mind–body interaction. In section 3 I pointed out that evolutionary biology shows the transition from animal to human to be too gradual to make sense of the idea that we humans have souls

---

[22] For a more extensive account of the theological issues involved in Darwin's thought and for a theological response, see my chapter "Science and Society," in James W. McClendon, Jr., ed., *Witness: Systematic Theology, Volume 3* (Nashville, TN: Abingdon Press, 2000), 99–131.

while animals do not. I also tried to expose several faulty reasons for *wanting* to distinguish ourselves from animals.

Now I turn to what I take to be the most decisive scientific contribution to the question of the make-up of the human person: the cognitive neurosciences. My argument in brief is this: all of the human capacities once attributed to the mind or soul are now being fruitfully studied as brain processes – or, more accurately, I should say, processes involving the brain, the rest of the nervous system and other bodily systems, all interacting with the socio-cultural world.

In chapter 1, I mentioned that contemporary people tend not to have precise notions of what the soul is, how it relates to mind, and so forth. Thus, I turn to the account developed by Thomas Aquinas. His is, I believe, the most elaborate and insightful theory in the Christian tradition.[23]

4.1 Biology and the life principle

What, according to Thomas, is the soul? In the first instance it is simply the life principle. Our word "animate" comes from the Latin for soul, *anima*. The question of what makes something alive is now handled by biology, and *how* it is handled is very instructive. Biologists and other natural scientists conceive of things in the universe as fitting into a hierarchy; not the medieval chain of being, but rather a hierarchy of complexity. The levels of complexity correspond roughly to the various sciences. Physicists study the lowest levels, the ultimate constituents of reality and their behavior in relatively simple systems, including atoms. Chemists study atoms in combination; biochemists study immensely complex molecules. Biology is multi-layered, studying macro-molecules, cells, tissues,

---

[23] Thomas's account is found primarily in his *Summa Theologiae*, part I, articles 75–102. In what follows I shall make use of Timothy McDermott's translation and edition, *Summa Theologiae: A Concise Translation* (Westminster, MD: Christian Classics, 1989), chapter 5.

organs, entire organisms, and ecosystems. In this hierarchy, new properties emerge. For example, there are properties of molecules that are entirely different from those of their components.

In the early years of the twentieth century there was a controversy in the philosophy of biology between vitalists and emergentists. The vitalists took an Aristotelian line: there must be something – a vital force – to direct the formation of an organism and to account for its being alive. The emergentists replied that all one needed was the proper functioning of a suitably complex entity and it would be alive. Life is an emergent property that is dependent on complex organization, not on an additional entity or non-material stuff. So this was the last gasp of the ancient and medieval idea of the soul as a life force.

Biologists today ask what the minimum requirements are for life. The basics are self-maintenance, growth, and reproduction. Thus, a sphere of proteins and other large molecules is living if, first, it has a membrane separating it from its environment; second, the membrane is permeable enough to allow for intake of nutrients; third, it has the ability to repair itself if damaged; and fourth, the ability to reproduce, even if only by splitting into two spheres, each of which grows large enough to split again. Note that the three functions Thomas attributed to the vegetative soul were growth, nutrition, and reproduction. The one feature he failed to note was self-repair.

The physicalist thesis is that as we go up the hierarchy of increasingly complex organisms, all of the other capacities once attributed to the soul will also turn out to be products of complex organization, rather than properties of a non-material entity.

4.2 Neuroscience and the animal soul

The faculties Thomas attributed to the animal or sensitive soul were locomotion, appetite, sensation, and emotion. Let us consider these in turn.

Thomas's (and Aristotle's) distinction between plant and animal on the basis of the ability to move from one place to another is still accepted.[24] The earliest and simplest form of locomotion is found in single-celled organisms equipped with flagella, fine whip-like structures on the surface of the cells that rotate and drive the cell forward. Such cells in a gradient of nutrients (or toxins) swim toward (or away from) higher concentrations. The mechanism is as follows: periodically the swimming cells randomly switch directions. In a favorable milieu they change less frequently and in an unfavorable milieu they change more frequently.[25] We have here the first hint of cognition, in that the organism is able to sense its environment and alter its behavior accordingly. So the connection between (primitive) sentience and locomotion appears even at this very low level of complexity.

A tremendous leap in complexity occurred with multicellular organisms, which allowed for the specialization of cell types. A particularly important cell type is the neuron. Before neurons developed, multi-celled organisms sent signals from one part to another by means of the diffusion of chemicals from one cell to others. The speed of such signaling was greatly enhanced by the development of cells with long fibers making a network throughout the body. "Cephalization" refers to the concentration of sensory and control functions at the anterior end of the organism.

In humans and other higher animals locomotion is controlled by a strip of cortex across the top of the brain, appropriately labeled the motor cortex, and by subcortical regions. These brain regions direct muscle movements by means of the efferent nervous system, and the

---

[24] I once heard a lecturer describe a marine organism on the borderline between plant and animal. It spends most of its time attached to rocks, but during one phase of its life it develops a very simple brain, detaches from the rock, and moves to an area with more nutrients. Then it re-attaches and consumes its own brain. The lecturer likened it to a professor who had gotten tenure.

[25] Harold J. Morowitz, *The Emergence of Everything: How the World Became Complex* (Oxford: Oxford University Press, 2002), 101.

brain continually receives feedback from the body regarding its position and movements.

Thomas distinguished two sorts of appetite. The sort we share with animals is that which is directed toward sensible objects such as food or mates. Sense-appetite includes a pleasure-seeking drive that inclines animals (and humans) to pursue what pleases their senses and avoid what hurts them. It also includes an aggressive drive that inclines them to resist threats. The aggressive drive is the source of the emotion of anger.[26] We have already seen that even the most primitive organisms have mechanisms that move them away from environmental threats. Biologist Harold Morowitz says: "The basic emerging features of animalness are sensory organs, a nervous system, and a digestive tract."[27] So the pursuit of food is a given for animals. In higher animals it is mediated by the pleasure centers of the brain and is dependent upon a balance of neurotransmitters – the chemicals that facilitate transmission of impulses from one nerve to another. Sexual desire is highly dependent on hormones. The hormone oxytocin is secreted by the posterior pituitary gland in mammals during sexual intercourse and breast feeding. It has been found to be a significant factor in pair bonding in animals, and facilitates mother–infant bonding in humans.

A great deal of research has been done on the role of the brain and extended nervous system in sense perception. For example, visual perception in higher animals has developed from single, light-sensitive cells in primitive organisms. In human vision, signals are transmitted from two different kinds of light-sensitive cells in the retina, through a series of processors, to the visual cortex. The striking difference between lower and higher animals is that while the lower ones can respond to stimuli in their environments, they do so without knowing what they are doing – they lack consciousness.

[26] McDermott, ed., *Summa*, 125.   [27] Morowitz, *The Emergence of Everything*, 107.

There is a phenomenon called blind-sight that helps to make clear the difference between conscious and non-conscious perception. Certain victims of damage to the visual cortex are either completely blind or have blind spots in their visual fields. Nonetheless, they are receiving information about their environments. If they are asked to say where an object is they will reply that they do not know, but if told to reach for it they do much better than would be expected by chance.[28] So the value of consciousness is that we not only know things about our environment, but we also know that we know.

How consciousness arises from brain function is, as neuroscientists say, the hard problem. There are two prominent attitudes in current literature regarding consciousness. One is well represented by the title of philosopher Daniel Dennett's book, *Consciousness Explained*.[29] The other view is that of philosophers such as Thomas Nagel,[30] designated by their opponents as the "new mysterians,"[31] who claim that consciousness is essentially inexplicable. A middle position might be more reasonable. In previous centuries life was as mysterious as consciousness is now. As just noted, it was thought that it could only be explained by invoking a soul or vital force. However, in recent years it has been possible to study ever simpler life forms and to list the minimal ingredients that go into the distinction between the living and the non-living.[32] The fact that we can observe the continuities between simplest life forms and non-living predecessors, on the one hand, and between those simple forms and increasingly complex organisms on the other gives us a

---

[28] See Lawrence Weiskrantz, *Consciousness Lost and Found: A Neuropsychological Exploration* (New York: Oxford University Press, 1997).

[29] Daniel C. Dennett, *Consciousness Explained* (Boston: Little, Brown, and Co., 1991).

[30] Thomas Nagel, *Mortal Questions* (London: Cambridge University Press, 1979).

[31] Owen Flanagan apparently coined this term.

[32] Gail Raney Fleishaker, "Three Models of a Minimal Cell," in C. Ponnamperuma and F. R. Erlich, eds., *Prebiotic Self Organization of Matter* (n.p.p.: A. Deepak Publishing, 1990), 235.

sense of *understanding* life, as well as of being able to list its necessary and sufficient conditions.

Approaches like Dennett's try to list the necessary and sufficient conditions for consciousness. In order to have a sense of *understanding* how consciousness can arise we might need to survey the spectrum from the first rudimentary form of sentience up to our own. Unfortunately, whereas it *is* possible to study simpler life forms "from the outside" and learn their biological features, it is *not* possible to study simpler life forms "from the inside," experiencing their more primitive forms of consciousness. The question, then, is whether it is possible in imagination to retrace the steps from the beginning and thus to de-mystify consciousness.

Back to Thomas Aquinas: in addition to the five "exterior" senses, Thomas postulated four "interior senses." These are particularly interesting in that they show Thomas's skill as a cognitive scientist and also link up with quite detailed work in neuroscience. These are attributes shared with higher animals. There are precursors of Thomas's views to be found in Aristotle, but largely Thomas borrowed here from Muslim scholar Ibn Sina.[33] Here is Timothy McDermott's contemporary translation of Thomas's account:

> Higher animals must be aware of something not only when it is present to their senses but also in its absence, so that they can be prompted to seek it. So they not only need to receive, but also to retain, impressions of sense objects presently affecting them.[34]

This ability to retain sense impressions in the absence of the stimulus is the interior sense called the *phantasia* in Latin, and often translated as "imagination."

> In addition, animals need to be attracted and repelled not only by what pleases or displeases their senses but by what is useful or

---

[33] Shams C. Inati, "Soul in Islamic Philosophy," in Edward Craig, ed., *Routledge Encyclopedia of Philosophy* (London and New York, 1998), vol. 9, p. 41.

[34] McDermott, *Summa*, 121; from Thomas's part I, article 78.

harmful in other ways: the straws birds collect must look good for nest-building. So animals must be able to perceive a significance in things that is not merely an externally perceptible quality. In addition to their particular senses ... for receiving sense impressions and their imagination for storing them, animals must therefore have an instinctive judgment [the *vis aestimativa*; also translated as "estimative power"] ... and a memory [*vis memorativa*, or "sense memory"] for storing those (for what is memorable to animals is what is harmful or agreeable and pastness itself is important to them in this way) ... Particular senses discern the particular sense-stimuli proper to them, but to distinguish white from sweet we need some common root sensitivity in which all sense-perceptions meet [the *sensus communis* – the "common" or "unifying sense"], and where we can perceive perception itself and become aware that we see.[35]

In this last sentence Thomas is raising the issue of consciousness itself.

An important question in neuroscience has been the controversy over how the brain comes to recognize patterns. Do brains come equipped with individual neurons designed for recognizing patterns – that is, a "grandmother neuron" devoted to recognition of this one particular elderly woman, and other cells for each pattern that the brain is able to distinguish? It is now believed that recognition tasks depend on activation of large nets or assemblies of neurons rather than on the firing of individual neurons. The concept of a "cell assembly" was introduced by Donald Hebb, and its formation is described as follows: "Any frequently repeated, particular stimulation will lead to the slow development of a 'cell-assembly,' a diffuse structure comprising cells ... capable of acting briefly as a closed system."[36] This issue is clearly relevant to an understanding of

---

[35] Ibid.
[36] Quoted in Alwyn Scott, *Stairway to the Mind: The Controversial New Science of Consciousness* (New York: Springer Verlag, 1995), 81.

Thomas's *phantasia* in that it is the re-activation of such an assembly that accounts for memory of the original set of stimuli.

In contemporary neuroscience, an explanation for Thomas's *sensus communis* is referred to as the binding problem, and it is considered one of the most difficult problems in current research, second only to the problem of consciousness itself.

Thomas's *vis aestimativa* is a particularly interesting faculty from the point of view of neuroscientific investigations. Neuroscientist Joseph LeDoux is well known for his investigations of emotion. What he writes about "emotional appraisal" is relevant to distinguishing this estimative power from the *sensus communis*:

> When a certain region of the brain is damaged [namely, the temporal lobe], animals or humans lose the capacity to appraise the emotional significance of certain stimuli [but] without any loss in the capacity to perceive the stimuli as objects. The perceptual representation of an object and the evaluation of the significance of an object are separately processed in the brain. [In fact] the emotional meaning of a stimulus can begin to be appraised before the perceptual systems have fully processed the stimulus. It is, indeed, possible for your brain to know that something is good or bad before it knows exactly what it is.[37]

So in Thomas's terms, the *vis aestimativa* is a separate faculty from the *sensus communis*, and it works faster.

Thomas emphasized that the *vis aestimativa* is also capable of recognizing intentions. Neuroscientist Leslie Brothers has contributed to an understanding of the neural basis for such recognition in both humans and animals. Humans and other social animals come equipped with neural systems that predispose them to pick out faces. The amygdala has been shown to be necessary for

---

[37] Joseph LeDoux, *The Emotional Brain: The Mysterious Underpinnings of Emotional Life* (New York: Simon and Schuster, 1996), 69.

interpreting facial expressions, direction of gaze, and tone of voice. Brothers has shown that neurons in the same region are responsive to the sight of hands and of leg motions typical of walking. Thus, there are particular neurons whose function is to respond to visual stimuli that indicate the intentions of other agents.[38]

LeDoux's research is also relevant to Thomas's *vis memorativa*, the ability to remember the emotional significance of a stimulus. He tells of a patient of a French physician named Edouard Claparede, who had apparently lost all of her abilities to create new memories as a result of brain damage. LeDoux reports:

> Each time Claparede walked into the room he had to reintroduce himself to her, as she had no recollection of having seen him before ... One day, he tried something new. He entered the room, and, as on every other day, he held out his hand to greet her. In typical fashion she shook his hand. But when their hands met, she quickly pulled hers back, for Claparede had concealed a tack in his palm and had pricked her with it. The next time he returned to the room to greet her, she still had no recognition of him, but she refused to shake his hand ... [but] could not tell him why ... Claparede had come to signify danger. He was no longer just a man ... but had become a stimulus with a specific emotional meaning ... [S]he learned that Claparede's hand could cause her harm, and her brain used this stored information, this memory, to prevent the unpleasantness from occurring again.[39]

By investigating fear conditioning in rats, LeDoux has confirmed the crucial role of the amygdala, a distinctive cluster of neurons found in the anterior temporal lobe of each hemisphere, in developing this sort of memory.

---

[38] Leslie Brothers, *Friday's Footprint: How Society Shapes the Human Mind* (New York and Oxford: Oxford University Press, 1997), chapter 3.
[39] LeDoux, *The Emotional Brain*, 180f.

4.3 Investigating the rational soul

For Thomas the rational soul is what makes us distinctively human. He attributed to it two sorts of intellect, passive and active, and will. The active intellect is the power humans have, but not animals, of acquiring abstract information from sense experience and forming judgments. Its capacities are expressed primarily in the use of language. Passive intellect is a kind of memory – a memory of facts and ideas. Memory of events Thomas attributed to the sensitive part of the soul.

Neuroscientists now distinguish something like a dozen different memory systems. The two sorts of memory that Thomas distinguished are both classified as types of declarative memory and involve the medial temporal lobe of the brain. The *formation* of long-term memory requires the functioning of the hippocampus.

The functions Thomas attributed to the active intellect – abstraction, judgment, and reasoning – are less well understood in neurobiological terms than are the faculties shared with animals. However, all of these higher human capacities depend on language and a great deal of work has been done on the neural bases of language use. This is a two-step process: first the cognitive capacities that go into language use, such as knowledge of meanings and recall of the sounds of words, need to be identified. Second, this "cognitive architecture" needs to be mapped onto the brain. Two regions of the brain have long been known to be involved in language use: Wernicke's area and Broca's area. Neuroscientist Peter Hagoort summarizes the data from fifty brain imaging studies that mapped the regions involved in the simple task of producing a single word.

All core steps in the speaking process are subserved by areas in the left hemisphere, which is the language dominant hemisphere in the large majority of people. Selecting the appropriate concept for speaking . . . seems to involve the left medial temporal gyrus. From there the activation spreads to Wernicke's area, which is pivotal in retrieving the phonological code of a word stored in memory. Wernicke's area plays a crucial role in the whole network of language processing by linking the lexical aspects of a word form to the widely distributed associations that define its meaning. This role is played by Wernicke's area in both language production and language comprehension. The lexical word form information is relayed to Broca's area in the left frontal cortex and/or the middle part of the superior temporal lobe in the left hemisphere. These areas play a role in the conversion of the phonological codes in memory into phonological words from which the abstract articulatory program is derived. In the final phase of preparing for articulation and execution of articulation sensorimotor areas become activated, with the possible additional contribution of the supplementary motor area and the cerebellum . . .[40]

So we can see the beginning of an understanding of the very complex brain processes that enable us to engage in language-based reasoning.

The third of Thomas's rational faculties was the will. This is the capacity to be attracted to goods of a non-sensory sort. As Anthony Kenny says, the will is "a power to have wants that only the intellect can frame . . . We can say roughly that the human will is the power to have those wants which only a language-user can have."[41] Along with intellect, this is the seat of moral capacities. Furthermore, since God is the ultimate good, the will also accounts for the capacity to be attracted to God.

Neuroscience now contributes to our understanding of both morality and religious experience. Antonio Damasio has studied

---

[40] Peter Hagoort, "The Uniquely Human Capacity for Language Communication: From *POPE* to [po:p] in Half a Second," in Robert Russell *et al.*, eds., *Neuroscience and the Person: Scientific Perspectives on Divine Action* (Vatican City State and Berkeley, CA: Vatican Observatory and Center for Theology and the Natural Sciences, 1999), 45–56.

[41] Anthony Kenny, *Aquinas on Mind* (London and New York: Routledge, 1993), 59.

the neural processes that go into practical reasoning, that is, the ability to make both moral and prudential judgments. In his book, *Descartes' Error*, he reports the case of a nineteenth-century railway worker, Phineas Gage, whose brain was pierced by a metal rod. Gage recovered physically and his cognitive functions (attention, perception, memory, reasoning, language) were all intact. Yet he suffered a dramatic character change after the accident. The doctor who treated him noted that he had become "fitful, irreverent, indulging at times in the grossest profanity which was not previously his custom, manifesting but little deference for his fellows, impatient of restraint or advice when it conflicts with his desires, at times pertinaciously obstinate, yet capricious and vacillating, devising many plans of future operation, which are no sooner arranged than they are abandoned."[42] Hanna Damasio was able to determine from the damage to Gage's skull exactly which parts of the brain would have been destroyed in the accident – selected areas of his prefrontal cortices. The Damasios conclude from this and other similar cases that this area of the brain is "concerned specifically with unique human properties, among them the ability to anticipate the future and plan accordingly within a complex social environment; the sense of responsibility toward the self and others; and the ability to orchestrate one's survival deliberately, at the command of one's free will."[43] In short, what Thomas described as the "appetite for the good" appears to depend directly on localizable brain functions.

A number of neuroscientists have begun to study the role of the brain in religious experience. For example, patients with temporal lobe epilepsy often develop strong interests in religion, and this has led to speculation that the temporal lobes are involved in certain sorts of *normal* religious experiences as well.[44] Andrew Newberg has

---

[42] Antonio Damasio, *Descartes' Error: Emotion, Reason, and the Human Brain* (New York: G. P. Putnam's Sons, 1994), 8.

[43] Ibid., 10.

[44] See, for example, Michael A. Persinger, *Neuropsychological Bases of God Beliefs* (New York: Praeger Publishers, 1987).

studied Buddhist monks during meditation and Franciscan nuns during prayer, and shows particular regions of the brain to be typically activated.[45] I am often asked to comment on these brain imaging studies; I always point out that if one is a physicalist, as I am, it is not surprising that brain regions are involved in religious experience – in fact some regions would have to be. I also try to point out that these studies say nothing about the existence or nonexistence of God. However, I have never found a better way to put it than neuropsychologist Malcolm Jeeves.

> Making inferences from brain states could become risky business. Consider, for example, the likely state of the brain of Sir Henry Wotton ... Wotton described fishing as "a rest to his mind, a cheerer of his spirits, a diverter of sadness, a calmer of unquiet thoughts, a moderator of passions, a procurer of contentedness ..." Such a description might suggest a brain state similar to some forms of religious meditation. However, it would be hazardous to suggest that because Sir Henry Wotton's selective brain activity resulted from his focus on fish, therefore it proved the existence of fish.[46]

Neither is brain imaging going to provide evidence for or against the existence and action of God.

In this section I have gone down one of the most detailed lists available of the human capacities that have been attributed to the soul, but I have barely scratched the surface of the neuroscientific work that has been done on each of these capabilities. Someone might object, though, that I have left out the most important thing about the soul – it is the part that goes to heaven. In my first lecture I suggested that Christians ought to think of the next life in terms of resurrection of the body rather than a soul departing for heaven.

---

[45] Andrew B. Newberg, Eugene d'Aquili, and V. Rause, *Why God Won't Go Away* (New York: Balantine, 2001).

[46] Malcolm Jeeves, "Changing Portraits of Human Nature," *Science & Christian Belief* 14, no. 1 (2002): 3–32.

Nonetheless, let us consider what characteristics your soul would have to retain for it to be recognizably *you* who gets to heaven. Your consciousness, your memories, your likes and dislikes, perhaps? But, as we have just seen, these are all the province of brain studies. I shall consider further the criteria for personal identity in chapter 4.

5. Retrospect and prospect

So what are we to make of all this? It is important to note that no such accumulation of data can ever amount to a proof that there is no immaterial mind or soul in addition to the body. But if we recognize that the soul was originally introduced into Western thought not from Hebraic Scripture but as an *explanation* for capacities that appeared not to be explainable in biological terms, then we can certainly say that for scientific purposes the hypothesis has been shown to be unnecessary. I shall pursue this issue further in chapter 4 (section 2). So biblical studies and neuroscience are both pointing in the same direction: toward a physicalist account of the person. Humans are not hybrids of matter and something else, they are purely physical organisms.

Note that it would be easy at this point to fall into the reductionist's error of claiming that the higher human capacities are *nothing but* brain processes. Reductionism is one of the central issues that I shall take up in the following chapters. There my task will be to develop a position called "nonreductive physicalism" and to contrast it with a reductive version of physicalism.

What do I mean by this? Let me try putting it this way: in the past, the soul served a variety of purposes, one of which was explanation of what we might call humans' higher capabilities. These capacities include a sort of rationality that goes beyond that of animals, as well as morality and a relationship with God. A reductive view would be to say that if there is no soul then people must not be truly rational, moral, or religious. What was taken in the past to be rationality, morality, and relationship with God is really nothing but brain processes. The nonreductive physicalist says instead that if there is no soul then these higher human capacities must be explained in a different manner. *In part* they are explainable as brain functions, but their *full* explanation requires attention to human social relations, to cultural factors, and, most importantly, to our relationship with God.

So take a particular human event – my writing this sentence, for example. Is what is going on in my brain right now an adequate explanation? Clearly not. Part of the explanation is the fact that I care about sharing my ideas with my readers. Why do I care about writing this book and doing it well? Part of the answer is that I recognized some years ago that I had a call from God to use my philosophical education for the sake of the church. So a complete explanation involves interactions with other people and the action of God in my life.

My goal in the next two chapters, then, is to address a few of the issues that divide reductionists and anti-reductionists. In chapter 3, I shall say more about reductionism in general and why it is, on the one hand, so clearly wrong, but on the other so difficult to escape. I shall then attempt to respond to the question of how a deterministic neural system can give rise to morally responsible action. Finally, I shall tackle the thorny problem of free will. In my fourth chapter, after a brief comment on philosophical method, I shall deal with the problems of human distinctiveness and of personal identity.

3 | Did my neurons make me do it? Reductionism, morality, and the problem of free will

1. Prospect

My two previous chapters have dealt with theories of human nature from the point of view, first, of theology and biblical studies, and second of science. I noted in chapter 1 that within the general population a view of humans as composed of body, soul, and spirit is often the preferred position. Equally popular is dualism, and there are two versions: body and soul or body and mind. Trichotomism and dualism are in conflict with majority views in neuroscience, where some sort of physicalism or materialism is the preferred view. This makes it appear that science and religion are headed for conflict. For example, Nobel-Prize-winning scientist Francis Crick claims to have falsified Christianity by showing that there is no soul. In contrast, I have argued that there is a remarkable convergence here between science and Christian scholarship. Christian scholars began to draw the same conclusion a hundred years ago. In fact, the body–soul dualism in Christian history has been more of an accommodation to culture than distinctive to biblical teaching.

I also pointed out in chapter 1 that there have been a variety of *philosophical* theories in Western history. In modern philosophy mind–body dualism has been a major contender for three hundred years, from René Descartes to Gilbert Ryle. Since the 1950s, though, the number of dualists has been decreasing and the number of physicalists has been increasing dramatically. The success of neuroscience in understanding mental processes through study of the brain, which I addressed in chapter 2, has been a significant factor. Another factor has been the growing conviction that mind–body interaction, as understood by modern dualists, is simply unintelligible. There are still a number of dualists among philosophers, and almost all of these appear to have theological motivations for defending dualism.

I certainly do not mean to criticize my fellow Christian philosophers for defending a position for theological reasons; in fact that is what I intend to do in the remainder of this volume. Christian philosophers have no need to defend dualism, but they *do* need to enter into debate with other physicalists in order to argue *against* reductionism. One way of understanding the difference between reductionist and nonreductionist versions of physicalism is stated by philosopher Mary Midgley. She says: "If certain confusions result from Descartes' having sliced humans down the middle, many people feel that the best cure is just to drop the immaterial half altogether . . ."[1] The problem with this form of physicalism is that it results in denial of the capacities and functions once attributted to the soul. The nonreductive physicalist makes no such denial, and instead seeks to show how all of these capacities depend on the body in its relations to the world, to culture, and to God. This will be the task of both this chapter and the next.

Two of the most daunting reductionist challenges are how to understand free will and moral responsibility. The reductionist says: "If humans are purely physical then their behavior *must* be determined by the laws of nature and therefore they cannot be free or morally responsible." Thus, the problem of free will, in this instance, is the problem of *avoiding* neurobiological reductionism.[2]

---

[1] Mary Midgley, "The Soul's Successors: Philosophy and the 'Body,'" in Sarah Coakley, ed., *Religion and the Body* (Cambridge: Cambridge University Press, 1997), 53–68.

[2] The problem of neurobiological reductionism is treated in more technical detail in Nancey Murphy and Warren S. Brown, *Did My Neurons Make Me Do It?* (forthcoming).

I shall take a two-pronged approach to this problem. First, I shall offer some arguments against causal reductionism in general. Causal reductionism hinges on the assumption that the behavior of the parts of an entity determines the behavior of the whole. Because the parts of an entity represent a *lower level* of complexity, this is called bottom-up causation. I shall argue that bottom-up causal factors often provide only a partial account of how things work. One also needs to consider holistic properties of the entity, as well as the interaction between the entity and its environment. Thus, I shall argue for top-down or downward causation; this is the thesis that factors at a higher level of complexity have causal influences on the entity's constituents.

The second prong of my attack will be to consider, step by step, the differences between machines and even the simplest organisms, on the one hand, and on the other, the differences between simple organisms and humans. We shall see that as we go up the hierarchy of complexity one finds increasing capacities for *self-direction*. Putting these two lines of thought together, I shall conclude that humans are highly self-directed organisms whose behavior exerts downward causal control over their own neural systems.

I then turn to the issue of morality. The problem is closely related to that of rationality: how humans come to govern their own behavior on the basis of *moral* reasons. I shall end by asking whether this account of morally responsible action offers all that one needs in terms of free will.

2. What's wrong with reductionism?

In chapter 2 I introduced two ideas that have been basic to the modern worldview. One of these is the atomistic metaphysical theory that serves as the basis of modern physics. Atomistic thinking soon spread to other disciplines and came to be so much taken for granted that it was often not argued or even stated. The basic idea is that the parts of an entity determine the behavior of the whole. Stewart Goetz makes a helpful distinction between "past-to-present determinism" – the view that a past state of the universe and relevant causal laws together entail the occurrence of one course of events – and "bottom-to-top determinism."[3] On this latter view, our commonsense notion that macroscopic objects (rocks, horses, people, for example) exert causal effects on one another is only a manner of speaking; all macroscopic past-to-present causation is in fact by means of micro-to-micro-causal processes. All of the real causal work is done at the lowest level. On this account, commonsense entities came to be seen as ontologically secondary when contrasted with the primary ontological status of the atoms.[4]

In chapter 2 I also introduced the idea of the hierarchy of complexity, mirrored by the hierarchy of the sciences – from physics up through chemistry and biology, and perhaps thence to psychology and the social sciences. These sciences each study increasingly complex systems, whose parts are made of the entities of the level below.

If we combine these two assumptions with the further assumption that the laws of nature are deterministic, it seems to follow that the behavior of any complex entity is determined by the laws governing the behavior of its parts, and ultimately by the laws of physics. In short:

1. All entities are (nothing but) arrangements of atoms.
2. Atoms have ontological priority over the entities they compose.
3. The laws of nature are deterministic.
4. Therefore the behavior of complex entities is determined by the behavior of their parts.
5. And therefore the laws of physics determine the behavior of all complex entities.

[3] Stewart Goetz, "Naturalism and Libertarian Agency," in William Lane Craig and J. P. Moreland, eds., *Naturalism: A Critical Analysis* (London and New York: Routledge, 2000), 156–186; 167f.
[4] Edward Pols, *Mind Regained* (Ithaca: Cornell University Press, 1998), 64.

This is the source of the causal-reductionist thesis. William Hasker expresses it well: "The only concrete existents involved [in putative cases of downward causation] are the ultimate constituents and combinations thereof; the only causal influences are those of the ultimate constituents in their interactions with each other . . ."[5]

2.1 The pervasive influence of pictures

Philosopher Ludwig Wittgenstein noted that we necessarily conceive the world by means of conceptual paradigms or pictures. Yet "[w]e do not judge the pictures, we judge by the pictures. We do not investigate them, we use them to investigate something else."[6] Wittgenstein took it to be a clue that one was in the grip of such a picture when one says "but it *must* be this way."[7] I have put a "must" on the reductionist's lips (in section 1) because I believe that modern thinkers have been in the grip of a picture or conceptual paradigm. If I am right that this is a worldview issue – a picture or conceptual paradigm in Wittgenstein's terms – then it is very difficult to mount an *argument* against it. It is so deeply ingrained in modern thought that it serves as a measure against which arguments are tested. Wittgenstein's recommendation in such cases is to "look and see." *Must* it be this way?

We cannot "look and see" whether human behavior is entirely determined by the laws of physics or neurobiology.[8] So let us look at

---

[5] William Hasker, *The Emergent Self* (Ithaca and London: Cornell University Press, 1999), 176.

[6] Ludwig Wittgenstein, *Remarks on the Foundations of Mathematics*, trans. G. E. M. Anscombe; ed. G. H. von Wright, Rush Rhees, and G. E. M. Anscombe (Cambridge: Cambridge University Press, 1978), IV § 12.

[7] Brad J. Kallenberg, *Ethics as Grammar: Changing the Postmodern Subject* (Notre Dame: University of Notre Dame, 2001), 199.

[8] The fact that the question can be phrased in terms of either physics or neurobiology is instructive. The degree to which quantum phenomena play a role in the brain is an open question, so it is unlikely that many serious thinkers believe that human behavior is governed directly by basic physics. In fact the Hodgkin–Huxley equations that govern

simpler cases. First, what does it mean to say that the lowest-level entities (the "atoms" in the philosophical sense of being "uncuttables" rather than in terms of current science) have "ontological priority"? One wants to say that it is only the atoms that are *really* real and everything else is *merely* a construction or arrangement of atoms. But what work is being done by the italicized words in the previous sentence? Consider two children playing with Legos. One (the anti-reductionist) says: "Look there's a house and a car and a dog and plane." The other (the reductionist) says: "No, all there *really* is is Legos." Is there any way to resolve this dispute? I suggest that there are two factors that weigh in on the side of the anti-reductionist. One is the extent to which the "new entities" are tightly interconnected and stable.[9] If all there is on the table is an outline of a house made of disconnected blocks, we might tend to agree with the reductionist. But if the house is solidly constructed and can be picked up and moved, we might tend to agree with the anti-reductionist.

The second factor is causation. If the new structures have causal capacities that the blocks alone do not have – if, for instance, the toy plane could fly – then, again, we might agree with the anti-reductionist. A typical answer to the philosophical question of how we decide what is real is to say that real things or properties are just the ones of which we need to take account in our causal interactions.

Of course a plane built of blocks cannot fly, and this brings us back to the question of whether there are things with genuinely new causal powers, or whether if we understood well enough how dogs and people are built we would see that their causal powers, like that of a real plane, are simply the product of the mechanical functioning of their parts, which in turn is determined by the laws of physics.

nerve impulse dynamics cannot be reduced to the laws of physics. (See Alwyn Scott, *Stairway to the Mind: The Controversial New Science of Consciousness* [New York: Springer-Verlag, 1995], 52–3.) If neural function cannot be derived from physics, why should we assume that human behavior can be derived from the laws of neurobiology?

[9] See Nancey Murphy and George F. R. Ellis, *On the Moral Nature of the Universe: Theology, Cosmology, and Ethics* (Minneapolis: Fortress Press, 1996), chapter 2.

Consider some further simple examples. First, a typical watch; it is designed so that its behavior is, as strictly as possible, determined by the behavior of its parts. Good watches are shock-proof and water-proof, and now not even dependent on the wearer remembering to wind them. Consider, though, a different kind of watch. I have one that re-sets itself every so often by picking up signals from orbiting satellites. It has been designed specifically so that its behavior is subject to readjustment by causal factors *from outside* the system.

Consider now a paper airplane. Its parts are the cellulose and other molecules making up the paper. These "parts" only serve the function of providing mass and rigidity. They do not do anything except be there. The behavior of the plane is almost entirely governed by two things: one is its shape – a holistic property of the plane. The other is environmental factors: the hand that throws it, and the air currents that affect its flight path. This ever-so-simple device shows that the atomist-reductionist thesis is simply false in some cases. So I should not have conceded above that the causal powers of a real plane are *simply* the product of its parts.

I suspect that there are readers who are wanting to say: "Yes, but the plane still obeys the laws of physics, so causation is still all bottom up." My reply is, first, to agree that the flight of the plane, once released, is determined by the laws of physics. Recall, though, that the question we were addressing is not the universal rule of the laws of nature, but rather the more specific question of whether the behavior of an entity is determined by the laws governing the behavior of its parts. All that I mean to show by this example is the falsity of this latter claim. What we find instead is evidence for three contrary points. First, the holistic property of the shape of the plane is crucial. Second, its behavior is a result of how this holistic property enables it to be affected by its environment, in ways that none of its parts alone could be. Third, although the flight of the plane is a result of air pressure, we might want to say that there are higher-level laws in effect (the laws of aerodynamics) which, while still counted as part of physics, are *emergent* in the sense that before there were things that fly or glide, there were no such regularities in the universe.[10] They are also emergent in the sense that they cannot be derived from quantum physics.[11]

2.2 Defending downward causation

What I am arguing, then, is for the applicability of the concept of downward or top-down causation. Accounts that consider only bottom-up causation – that is, the effect of the parts on the whole – are often inadequate. We also need to consider features of the whole as a whole, as well as the downward effects of the environment.

I believe that the most significant worry about the cogency of an account of downward causation is the problem of overdetermination: Where is there room for additional *downward* causal influences if the behavior of the lower-level entities is already determined by the laws of that level? How does downward causation *fail* to violate those laws? In the case of neurobiology, the question is, where is there room for downward influences if everything that happens in the brain is a product of the laws of neurobiology?

The concept of downward causation has been developing over the past half-century. Philosophical theologian Austin Farrer was clearly groping for such a concept in his 1957 Gifford Lectures. He argues that higher-level patterns of action may do some real work and thus not be reducible to the mass effect of lower-level constituents. For example, he says: "in cellular organization the molecular constituents are caught up and as it were bewitched by larger

---

[10] I recognize that this raises the question of the *nature* of the laws of nature: Are they merely descriptive of regularities in the universe or are they in some sense pre-existent and prescriptive?

[11] This section is adapted from my chapter titled "Nonreductive Physicalism," in Joel B. Green and Stuart L. Palmer, eds., *In Search of the Soul: Four Views of the Mind-Body Problem* (Downers Grove, IL: InterVarsity, 2005), 115–38.

patterns of action . . ."[12] Roger Sperry introduced the concept of top-down causation in psychology. In some cases he spoke of the properties of the higher-level entity or system *overpowering* the causal forces of the component entities.[13]

The question, then, is whether we can give an account of downward causation without having to suggest the bewitchment or overpowering of the lower-level laws. I suggest that we can, and doing so requires that we pay attention to some of the complexities of causal relations even at the level of physics. First, there is the distinction between laws and initial or boundary conditions. Pierre Simon de Laplace is the arch reductionist of modern physics. He expressed his determinist views in epistemological terms: an intelligence that knew all the laws of nature and the position of all the beings of which nature is composed would know all future states of the universe. With the advantage of hindsight, the beginning of the end of causal reductionism can be seen already in Laplace's determinism: *given* knowledge of the position of all of the particles in the universe, all future states could be deduced. That is, as neopositivist philosophers of science of the mid-twentieth-century pointed out, explanation of physical phenomena requires knowledge of both the laws governing transitions from one state to another and of the *antecedent* (or *initial* or *boundary*) conditions of the system. These terms are sometimes used interchangeably to refer both to states of a system S and to conditions of a larger system of which S is a part. To preserve this distinction without running foul of general usage I shall speak of structural conditions when I mean to refer to initial or boundary conditions of S and of environmental conditions when we refer to states of S's environment.

[12] Austin Farrer, *The Freedom of the Will*, The Gifford Lectures, 1957 (New York: Charles Scribner's Sons, 1958), 57. I assessed his contribution to these issues in "Downward Causation and *The Freedom of the Will*," paper presented at Austin Farrer Centenary Conference, Oxford, September 2004.
[13] Roger W. Sperry, *Science and Moral Priority: Merging Mind, Brain, and Human Values* (New York: Columbia University Press, 1983), 117.

Science, until recently, has focused on the laws and has taken structural and environmental conditions to be unproblematic. In fact, the success of experimental science has depended on scientists' ability to control or systematically vary the conditions in order to perceive regularities in the behavior of the entities in question. In simple systems regularities will appear despite a wide variety of conditions. For example, the acceleration of a body in free fall is the same within a wide range of sizes and shapes of the object. We can see, though, that it takes very little in the way of increased complexity to make both structural and environmental conditions critical. Consider the difference between a body in free fall and one rolling down an inclined plane. For the former, environmental conditions such as air density, and structural conditions such as the shape of the object, make negligible differences within a wide range of conditions. For an object rolling down an incline, however, the environmental conditions such as degree of tilt and smoothness of the surface make a great deal of difference, as does the shape of the object itself.

German philosopher of science Bernd-Olaf Küppers argues that the biological sciences have recently undergone a paradigm shift due to recognition that complex systems such as living organisms are extremely sensitive to structural and environmental conditions and, therefore, explanation of the causes of the conditions themselves is at least as important as investigation of the laws governing the processes that transpire within the organism. So the importance of the distinction between conditions and laws is that it provides a way of thinking about how top-down and bottom-up causation may be complementary: top-down determination of structural conditions is entirely compatible with the uninterrupted operation of lower-level laws once those structures are in place.[14]

---

[14] Bernd-Olaf Küppers, "Understanding Complexity," in Robert J. Russell, Nancey Murphy, and Arthur R. Peacocke, eds., *Chaos and Complexity: Scientific Perspectives on Divine Action* (Vatican City State and Berkeley, CA: Vatican Observatory and The Center for Theology and the Natural Sciences, 1995), 93–105.

Philosopher Fred Dretske has provided valuable terminology for understanding the relationship between causal laws and structural conditions. He distinguishes between triggering causes and structuring causes, as illustrated by the following example: "A terrorist plants a bomb in the general's car. The bomb sits there for days until the general gets in is car and turns the key . . . The bomb is detonated (triggered by turning the key in the ignition) and the general is killed." The terrorist's action was the structuring cause, the cause of its being the case that turning the key sets off the bomb.[15] Our previous example of a marble rolling down an incline will serve as another example. Cutting grooves in the surface is a structuring cause and determines, along with the law of gravity, the trajectory of the marble.

So for many purposes it is an oversimplification to represent a causal sequence simply as a series of events: $E_1 -> E_2 -> E_3$. Instead we need to think of *two* series of events: those leading up to the triggering of the effect and also those leading up to the condition under which the triggering cause is able to cause the effect. Dretske's account helps make clear what earlier theorists such as Sperry were attempting to articulate when they pointed out that the behavior of higher-level entities cannot be understood without taking into account the spatio-temporal patterning of physical masses, and when Sperry claimed, in addition, that such patterns exert causal influences in and of themselves.[16]

Philosopher of science Donald Campbell offered an account of downward causation at about the same time as Sperry. Campbell has crafted an account of how a larger system of causal factors can exert downward efficacy on lower-level entities by means of *selection*. His example is the role of natural selection in producing the

---

[15] Fred Dretske, "Mental Events as Structuring Causes of Behavior," in John Heil and Alfred Mele, eds., *Mental Causation* (Oxford: Clarendon Press, 1995), 121–136.

[16] Roger W. Sperry, "The Import and Promise of the Cognitive Revolution," *American Psychologist* 48, no. 8 (August 1993): 878–85.

remarkably efficient jaw structures of worker termites and ants. The jaw structure of each individual ant is (largely) determined bottom-up by genetics, but how did the ants come to have those particularly useful sets of genetic information? The answer, of course, is natural selection. Campbell says:

> biological evolution in its meandering exploration of segments of the universe encounters laws, operating as selective systems, which are not described by the laws of physics and inorganic chemistry, and which will not be described by the future substitutes for the present approximations of physics and inorganic chemistry ... Where natural selection operates through life and death at a higher level of organisation, the laws of the higher-level selective system determine in part the distribution of lower-level events and substances. Description of an intermediate-level phenomenon is not completed by describing its possibility and implementation in lower-level terms. Its presence, prevalence or distribution (all needed for a complete explanation of biological phenomena) will often require reference to laws at a higher level of organisation as well.[17]

The most helpful recent account of top-down causation is Robert Van Gulick's.[18] Van Gulick makes his points about top-down causation in the context of an argument for the nonreducibility of higher-level sciences. The reductionist, he says, will claim that the causal roles associated with special-science classifications are entirely derivative from the causal roles of the underlying physical constituents of the objects or events picked out by the special

---

[17] Ibid., 180.

[18] Robert Van Gulick, "Who's in Charge Here? And Who's Doing All the Work?" in Heil and Mele, eds., *Mental Causation*, 233–56. After completing this chapter I discovered an even more helpful, although much more technical treatment. Alicia Juarrero argues for the role of downward "constraints" in hierarchies of increasingly complex dynamical systems. See her *Dynamics in Action: Intentional Behavior as a Complex System* (Cambridge, MA: MIT Press, 1999).

sciences. Van Gulick replies that although the events and objects picked out by the special sciences are composites of physical constituents, the causal powers of such an object are not determined solely by the physical properties of its constituents and the laws of physics, but also by the *organization* of those constituents within the composite. And it is just such patterns of organization that are picked out by the predicates of the special sciences. Another way to make the same point is to say that physical outcomes are determined by the laws of physics together with initial and boundary conditions. Thus, Van Gulick concludes, "we can say that the causal powers of a composite object or event are determined in part by its higher-order (special science) properties and not solely by the physical properties of its constituents and the laws of physics."[19] The patterns of boundary conditions picked out by the special sciences have downward causal efficacy in that they can affect which causal powers of their constituents are activated or likely to be activated.

> A given physical constituent may have many causal powers, but only some subsets of them will be active in a given situation. The larger context (i.e. the pattern) of which it is a part may affect which of its causal powers get activated ... Thus the whole is not any simple function of its parts, since the whole at least partially determines what contributions are made by its parts.[20]

Here we see a generalization of Campbell's insight that downward causation is not overpowering but selective activation of lower-level causal processes.

One of the best examples of downward causation via selection is the effect of the environment on a developing brain. Many theories of brain function rely on some form of "neural Darwinism."[21] That is, the answer to the question of how neural nets or cell assemblies

---

[19] Ibid., 251.   [20] Ibid.

[21] See, for instance, Gerald M. Edelman, *Bright Air, Brilliant Fire: On the Matter of the Mind* (New York: Harper Collins, 1992).

form is by a process of random growth of dendrites and synaptic connections, followed by selective reinforcement of connections that turn out to be useful. The best theory seems to be that co-presentation of stimuli to two neurons or groups of neurons, resulting in simultaneous activation of their respective receptors, strengthens neuronal connections between those receptors, making it more and more likely that both cells or groups of cells will fire when one is stimulated. So useful connections are strengthened, while unused connections weaken or die off. In this way, neural connections that model relations of various sorts in the world come to be selected.

2.3 Further complications

A great deal more could be said about the complexities of causal patterns and the ways in which these complexities leave room for downward causation. There are issues such as information flow, feedback mechanisms, nonlinear systems, self-sustaining and self-modifying systems.[22] Rather than pursue these in the abstract, consider another example: a jet-liner flying on auto-pilot. We have here a case where proper functioning of parts is critical, but as with the paper airplane the holistic features of mass and shape are critical, as well as its interaction with the environment – air turbulence, headwinds, and so on.

What is different about the jet-liner is the extent to which it is self-directed. Its behavior is self-determined and directed toward a goal. This is not, of course, a suitable analogue of human free will since the goal was predetermined by something outside of the system itself. In fact, the last thing we want is a plane that thinks for itself! My purpose here is only to call attention to the fact that it is possible to design a system that uses information about its own states and about its environment in such a way as to alter its own behavior in

---

[22] See Alwyn Scott, *Stairway to the Mind*; and Alicia Juarrero, *Dynamics in Action*.

pursuit of a goal. Once such systems have come into existence, new regularities, new laws of nature, come into existence with them. The basic laws of physics are not violated in such cases, and in fact it is the reliable working of the basic laws of physics that makes the design and operation of such systems possible.

3. The emergence of self-direction[23]

The purpose of this section is to build on the previous section's account of causal complexities by looking at organisms – in particular to consider the capacity noted in the jet-liner of a degree of self-direction. All living organisms are intrinsically active and goal-directed, at least to the extent that they pursue the goals of survival and reproduction. The jet's goals have been set by something outside the system, and the goals of primitive life forms are also predetermined, but in this case it is by natural selection. By the end of this section we shall see how complex organisms come to have the ability to modify their own goals.

I claimed in chapter 2 that life appears when there is a bounded organic structure capable of taking nutrients from the environment for the purposes of self-repair, growth, and reproduction. Biologist Harold Morowitz speculates that life began with relatively simple "protocells" capable of replication.[24] The first *known* organisms are the prokaryotes such as bacteria, capable of very simple forms of metabolism. Somewhere in bacterial evolution motility appeared: flagella rotate and drive the cell forward. As already noted, cells in a gradient of nutrients swim toward higher concentrations, and in a gradient of toxins swim toward lower concentrations. So even at the level of

---

[23] I am using the term "emergence" here in a non-technical sense. For an evaluation of technical uses of the concept, see Nancey Murphy and William R. Stoeger, S. J., eds., *Emergence: From Physics to Theology* (Oxford: Oxford University Press, forthcoming).

[24] Harold J. Morowitz, *The Emergence of Everything: How the World Became Complex* (Oxford: Oxford University Press, 2002), 29.

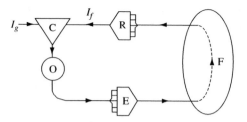

Figure 3.1. Diagram representing the components of a simple self-governing, goal-directed system.

single-celled organisms we find a degree of self-direction. Morowitz says "the behavior looks causal but the end point looks teleological."[25] We have here the first hint of cognition, in that the organism is able to sense its environment and alter its behavior accordingly.

A crucial ingredient in self-direction toward a goal is the ability to use information for redirecting the system's activity. Donald MacKay was a physicist who contributed to the development of information theory and then moved into the field of neuroscience. His approach to the understanding of cognition is in terms of information-processing systems. In engineering terms our mobile bacterium is a system governed by a feedback loop. The first mechanical system of this sort was designed by James Watt in the days of steam locomotives. A more familiar example is a thermostatically controlled heating system. All simple self-governing systems can be represented by a diagram as in Figure 3.1.

Here the action of the effector system, E, in the field, F, is monitored by the receptor system, R, which provides an indication, I_f, of the state of F. This indication is compared with the goal criterion, I_g, in the comparator, C, which informs the organizing system, O, of any mismatch. O selects from the repertoire of E action calculated to reduce the mismatch.[26]

[25] Ibid., 102.

[26] Donald M. MacKay, *Behind the Eye*, The Gifford Lectures, ed. Valerie MacKay (Oxford: Basil Blackwell, 1991), 43–4.

A crucially important feature of even rudimentary biological activity, then, is action under evaluation. In most cases this is not conscious evaluation, but only a system that is able to correct the routine when feedback from the environment indicates a mismatch between the behavioral routine and the goals, as in the case of the bacterium mentioned above. Different degrees of cognitive power lead to differing degrees of flexibility in responding to the mismatch.

3.1 Fixed patterns of complex activity

Insects exhibit forms of complex activity that are fixed rather than flexible. A fine example is the *Sphex ichneumoneus*, a type of wasp, now beloved insect of the philosophical literature.

When the time comes for egg laying, the wasp *Sphex* builds a burrow for the purpose and seeks out a cricket which she stings in such a way as to paralyze but not kill it. She drags the cricket into the burrow, lays her eggs alongside, closes the burrow, then flies away, never to return. In due course, the eggs hatch and the wasp grubs feed off the paralyzed cricket, which has not decayed, having been kept in the wasp equivalent of deep freeze. To the human mind, such an elaborately organized and seemingly purposeful routine conveys a convincing flavor of logic and thoughtfulness – until more details are examined. For example, the wasp's routine is to bring the paralyzed cricket to the burrow, leave it on the threshold, go inside to see that all is well, emerge, and then drag the cricket in. If the cricket is moved a few inches away while the wasp is inside making her preliminary inspection, the wasp, on emerging from the burrow, will bring the cricket back to the threshold, but not inside, and will then repeat the preparatory procedure of entering the burrow to see that everything is all right. If again the cricket is removed a few inches while the wasp is inside, once again she will move the cricket up to the threshold and re-enter the burrow for a final check. The wasp never thinks of pulling the cricket straight in. On one occasion this procedure was repeated forty times, always with the same result.[27]

Thus, the behavior of *Sphex* is fixed in a predetermined pattern in relationship to specific environmental clues. Her response is hard-wired and cannot be adapted to devilment by the entomologist.

3.2 Mammalian flexibility

Mammals exhibit much more flexibility in responding to their environments. They have the ability to suspend the pursuit of one goal, such as getting a drink of water, for the sake of a more pressing goal, such as avoiding a predator. Animals are capable of learning by trial and error and by imitation. Even so, our closest animal relative, the chimpanzee, is incapable of the same kind of flexibility that we see in small children.

Terrence Deacon describes an instructive series of experiments with chimpanzees. A chimpanzee is given the opportunity to choose between two unequal piles of candy; it always chooses the bigger one. Then the situation is made more complicated: the chimpanzee chooses, but the experimenter gives the chosen pile to a second chimpanzee and the first ends up with the smaller one. Children over the age of two catch on quickly and choose the smaller pile. But chimpanzees have a very hard time catching on; they watch in agitated dismay, over and over, as the larger pile of candy is given away.

Deacon says that the task poses a difficulty for the chimpanzees because the presence of such a salient reward undermines their ability to stand back from the situation and subjugate their desire to the pragmatic context, which requires them to do the opposite of what they would normally do to achieve the same end.

Now the experiment is further complicated. The chimpanzees are taught to associate numbers with the piles of candy. When given the

---

[27] D. Woolridge, *Mechanical Man: The Physical Basis of Intelligent Life* (New York: McGraw Hill, 1968), 82.

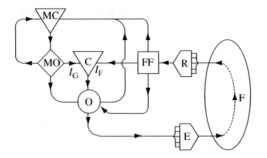

Figure 3.2. Diagram representing a self-governing system with the ability to reset its own goals.

chance to select numbers rather than the piles themselves, they quickly learn to choose the number associated with the smaller pile. Deacon argues that the symbolic representation helps reduce the power of the stimulus to drive behavior. Thus, he argues that increasing ability to create symbols progressively frees responses from stimulus-driven immediacy.[28]

The experiments with the chimpanzees illustrate another crucial ingredient in the escape from biological determinism. What the chimpanzees in the first phase of the experiment are unable to do is to make their own behavior, their own cognitive strategy, the object of their attention. This ability to represent to oneself aspects of one's own cognitive processes in order to be able to evaluate them is what I shall call self-transcendence. To represent this capacity we need a more complex diagram, as in Figure 3.2.

This figure represents a goal-seeking system (as in Figure 3.1) with an added feature, a supervisory system that takes stock of how things are going in the total system; it is represented in Figure 3.2 by two components, the meta-comparator, MC, and the meta-organizing system, MO. FF represents a feedforward part with feature filters that draw relevant information from sensory input for updating the organizing

---

[28] Terrence W. Deacon, *The Symbolic Species: The Co-evolution of Language and the Brain* (New York: W. W. Norton, 1997), 413–15.

system.[29] Such a system has the capacity to alter its own goal state in light of its evaluation of how the total system is coping with its environment.

Philosopher Daniel Dennett points out that the truly explosive advance in the escape from crude biological determinism comes when the capacity for pattern recognition is turned in upon itself. The creature who is not only sensitive to patterns in its environment, but also to patterns in its own reactions to patterns in its environment, has taken a major step.[30] Dennett's term for this ability is to "go meta" – one represents one's representations, reacts to one's reactions. "The power to iterate one's powers in this way, to apply whatever tricks one has to one's existing tricks, is a well-recognized breakthrough in many domains: a cascade of processes leading from stupid to sophisticated activity."[31]

4. Human self-determination and responsibility

Let us review the territory covered so far. In section 2 I have shown how to make room for environmental (that is, downward) causal influences in a law-governed system. There is room for downward causation to set up the initial conditions, including the structures within which the laws of the lower level operate. Often this is by means of selection of lower-level entities or causal processes according to the way they fit into higher-level causal systems.

I ended section 2 with the example of a system (the jet-liner) that was designed by humans to have a degree of self-direction. Entities such as guided missiles and jets become causal players in their own right when they are designed to respond to environmental conditions in such a way as to pursue a goal. In section 3 I traced the increasing cognitive

[29] MacKay, *Behind the Eye*, 141.
[30] Daniel C. Dennett, *Elbow Room: Varieties of Free Will Worth Wanting* (Cambridge, MA: MIT Press, 1984), 29; referring to D. R. Hofstadter, "Can Creativity Be Mechanized?" *Scientific American*, 247 (September 1982): 18–34.
[31] Dennett, *Elbow Room*, 29.

abilities in animals that give them increasing degrees of flexibility in responding to their own needs and to environmental influences. I ended the section with the suggestion that *language* and *self-transcendence* are the keys to escaping biological determinism.

The task of the remainder of this chapter is to consider what needs to be added to the account provided so far in order to conclude that humans have free will. However, I believe that the philosophical literature on free will contains a number of unhelpful starting points, so rather than ask first how the concept should be understood, let us consider what the purposes are for wanting to argue for human free will in the first place. The most important issue is the defense of moral responsibility, both for the sake of social issues such as meting out rewards and punishments and for the sake of our accountability before God. Consequently, my purpose in this section will be to build a case for moral responsibility that shows it to be compatible with what we know so far about cognition and neuroscience. My method will be to provide a list of the cognitive abilities that are prerequisites for moral responsibility and to suggest that these abilities arise out of our complex neural systems, interacting with the environment, both natural and social. In the next section I hope to show that this approach from the direction of the cognitive neurosciences helps to clarify some of the philosophical discussions of free will.

The analysis of moral responsibility that I shall employ comes from Alasdair MacIntyre's delightful book titled *Dependent Rational Animals*. He describes action as morally responsible when it is the product of the evaluation of that which moves one to action in light of some concept of the good.[32] I need to unpack this definition and show that our capacity for moral responsibility is not *in spite of* the activity of neurons but *because of* our neural complexity.

We take humans, at a point in their cognitive development, to be morally responsible, but in no case do we attribute moral

---

[32] Alasdair MacIntyre, *Dependent Rational Animals: Why Human Beings Need the Virtues* (Chicago: Open Court, 1999), 53, 56.

responsibility to animals. MacIntyre has helpfully related his account of morally responsible action to a survey of the literature on the behavior of higher animals – his focus is on dolphins – so that we can see precisely what needs to be added in the human case.

4.1 Animal precursors

First and foremost, dolphins exhibit goal-directedness. Dolphin goals include food, mates, satisfaction of curiosity, play, affection. MacIntyre argues that lack of language is no reason to deny that dolphins act for reasons, which means that they have the capacity to make judgments about what actions are likely to produce desired results. I mentioned some relevant factors in chapter 2. There I reported on Thomas Aquinas's "interior senses," which we share with animals, and then described some of the neurobiological research that is relevant to these capacities. One is the ability to recognize what is dangerous, friendly, useful; another is the capacity to store these judgments in memory.

I also reported on Antonio Damasio's thesis of somatic markers. This was in connection with the report on Phineas Gage who, through brain damage, had lost the subtle emotional cues that ordinarily move us to do things that are good for us and to resist things that have caused us trouble in the past. So, in addition to inborn goals, we can suppose that the higher animals have the same capacity to learn from experience by means of the development of somatic markers. These subtle emotional cues indicate that an immediately contemplated activity is either good to enact or bad to enact.

A great step forward in the ability to evaluate one's own action is the capacity to run behavioral scenarios in the imagination. This allows for prediction of effects of the action without having to go through the costly process of trial and error. Higher animals appear to have some capacity for this. Here is an example from the chimpanzees at the Arnhem Zoo.

Each morning ... the keeper hoses out all the rubber tires in the enclosure and hangs them one by one on a horizontal log ... One day [a chimp named] Krom was interested in a tire in which the water had been retained. Unfortunately, this particular tire was at the end of the row, with six ... tires hanging in front of it. Krom pulled and pulled at the one she wanted ... for over ten minutes, ignored by everyone except ... Jakie, a seven-year-old male chimpanzee to whom Krom used to be ... a caretaker ...

Immediately after Krom gave up ... Jakie approached. Without hesitation he pushed the tires off the log, one by one ... beginning with the front one ... When he reached the last tire, he carefully removed it so that no water was lost and carried the tire straight to [Krom], where he placed it upright in front of her.[33]

This scene suggests that Jakie had the ability to imagine a solution to the problem that saved him from the process of trial and error. It also illustrates two additional capacities shared with animals: the first is Krom's ability to change goals in light of experience that indicates that the goal was unachievable or not worth the effort – we might call this the "sour grapes" capacity that Aesop in one of his fables attributed to foxes.

Jakie's behavior exhibited another cognitive ability called a theory of other minds – that is, the ability to recognize the feelings and likely thoughts of another. Children develop this ability anywhere between three and nine years of age.

4.2 Language and the prerequisites for morality

Human morality builds upon these complex capacities. Most of the additional requirements for responsibility and morality depend on sophisticated symbolic language. These requirements are, first, a

---

[33] Frans de Waal, *Good Natured: The Origins of Right and Wrong in Humans and Other Animals* (Cambridge, MA: Harvard University Press, 1996), 83.

sense of self; second, the ability to pursue abstract goals; and, third, the ability to evaluate that which moves one to act.

The term "self" is used in a variety of ways in psychology and philosophy and it would take an entire chapter to provide an analysis of the term and then to relate it all to brain science. So this will be merely a preliminary sketch. What is at issue here is not the question of what it means to *be* a self. Rather the issue is that of having a self-*concept*. Such a concept arises, first, from the ability early in life to distinguish between self and nonself and, second, from the development of a theory of mind, mentioned above. This allows for recognition of others in the environment who have bodies of their own as well as thoughts and feelings – thus being able to recognize myself as a member of the class of selves or persons. Research by Leslie Brothers shows that we come well equipped neurobiologically to develop and use what she calls the person concept. We have remarkable abilities to recognize faces and we have neurons that specialize in detecting bodily motions that indicate other actors' intentions.[34]

Patricia Churchland examines some of the multifarious uses of the self-concept and concludes that the issue can profitably be recast in terms of the self-representational capacities of the brain.

> In the brain, some networks are involved in representing things in the external world, such as the face of Groucho Marx or a looming bus. Other networks represent states of the body, such as its posture or its need for water. Some networks operate on other representations, yielding meta-representations such as knowing that my need to flee is more urgent that my need for water, knowing that John dislikes me, or remembering that John hit me. Neural networks engaged in integrating such meta-representations are probably the ones most relevant to questions about self-representation.

---

[34] Leslie A. Brothers, *Friday's Footprint: How Society Shapes the Human Mind* (New York: Oxford University Press, 1997), chapter 3.

94

Self-representations may be widely distributed across brain structures, coordinated only on an "as-needed" basis, and arranged in a loose and loopy hierarchy. We see the slow emergence and elaboration of self-representational capacities in children, and the tragic fading of these capacities in patients with dementia.[35]

Churchland goes on to report on the neural dependencies of some of our self-representational capacities: for example, representation of the internal milieu of the viscera via pathways to the brain stem and hypothalamus; autobiographical events via the medial temporal lobes; control of impulses via prefrontal lobe and limbic structures. Other capacities involved are the ability to represent a sequence of actions to take next and to represent where one is both in space–time and in the social order.

These various self-representational capacities can be teased apart by considering victims of illnesses in which some capacities are intact and other are poor or non-existent. For example, schizophrenics have good autobiographical memory but difficulty with the self/nonself boundaries so that they often attribute their own thoughts to an external agent.

In addition, Warren Brown argues that a personal, autobiographical memory forms the basis of a continuous personal identity. Human episodic memory is apt to be of greater scope and complexity due to the capacity of human language to preserve detail, and because of the remarkably expanded size and complexity of our frontal lobes.[36]

I was assuming a moment ago that sophisticated animals have the capacity to evaluate courses of action in light of salient goals by means of mental representations. The possession of language clearly augments human ability to do so. In addition to *imagining* a course

[35] Patricia S. Churchland, "Self-Representation in Nervous Systems," *Science*, 296 (April 2002): 308–10.

[36] Warren S. Brown, "Cognitive Contributions to Soul," in Brown, *et al.*, eds., *Whatever Happened to the Soul?* 116.

of action and depending on past experience to judge whether it will be effective in attaining the goal, humans can consider a much broader range of possible actions due to the ability to describe them in language. Sophisticated language also contributes to our abilities to predict consequences. For example, one can consider a whole class of actions – say, acts of aggression – and ask in more abstract terms what the usual consequences have been in the past.

One very significant step in the development of responsible action is the fact that language allows us to represent to ourselves and pursue *abstract* goals, such as justice. Recall (from chapter 2) that Aquinas distinguished two sorts of appetite: that directed toward sensible objects, which we share with animals, and that directed toward goods of a non-sensible nature, which he defined as the will. Language is the key to this difference. I mentioned some of the neurobiological prerequisites for language in chapter 2.

4.3 Language and self-transcendence

MacIntyre argues that moral responsibility depends not only on possession of the capacity for abstract concepts but also on a high level of syntactical competence. He states that the ability to pass judgment on one's own judgments is the mark of both rationality and voluntariness. This meta-level judgment requires a type of language that has the resources necessary for constructing sentences that contain as constituents a representation of the first-order judgment.[37] That is, mature human rationality develops when children attain the ability to consider why they are doing what they are doing, and then to raise the question of whether there might be better reasons for acting differently. This requires the linguistic capacity to be able to say something like the following: I wanted to smoke to impress my friends, but taking care of my health is more important.

[37] MacIntyre, *Dependent Rational Animals*, 53–4.

Children become independent *moral* reasoners when they can switch from acting to please parents or peers to acting on the basis of some abstract concept of the good; not just what seems good to me now, but what is good *per se*.[38] MacIntyre says: "In so evaluating my desires I stand back from them. I put some distance between them and myself *qua* practical reasoner, just because I invite the question both from myself and from others, of whether it is in fact good for me to act on this particular desire here and now."[39]

This is but one example of the way in which cognitive processes need to be understood in terms of hierarchical levels of processing such that higher cognitive levels influence lower levels, for example, by means of attention, expectancy, intention – and thus lower-level brain processes. Thus, the higher-order evaluation that one brings to bear by attending to one's own motives and reasons exerts a downward influence, possibly changing the decision and future action – and, of course, the neural bases of the decision and its implementation.[40]

Let us now see how the factors I have suggested as prerequisites for moral responsibility work together. These factors are: first, a concept of self; second, the ability to run behavioral scenarios and predict the outcome of possible actions; third, the capacity for self-transcendence; fourth, sophisticated enough language to make a description of that which moves me to act the subject of evaluation; fifth and finally, the ability to evaluate my prior reasons in light of the abstract concept of goodness as such. Here is how MacIntyre relates these capacities:

> as a practical reasoner I have to be able to imagine different possible futures *for me*, to imagine myself moving forward from the starting point of the present in different directions. For different or alternative futures present me with different and alternative sets of goods to be achieved, with different possible modes of flourishing. And it is

---

[38] Ibid., 71–2, 84. [39] Ibid., 69.
[40] Brown, "Cognitive Contributions to Soul," 118.

97

important that I should be able to envisage both nearer and more distant futures and to attach probabilities, even if only in a rough and ready way, to the future results of acting in one way rather than another. For this both knowledge and imagination are necessary.[41]

We can see that the ability to use sophisticated language makes it possible for social influences in the form of rewards and punishments, but especially in the form of abstract concepts such as justice and kindness, to exert a downward influence on one's means–end reasoning and actions by providing goals against which to evaluate one's plans for action. These abilities emerge slowly in human development, and thus it is right that societies do not hold children and those with diminished reasoning capacity responsible for their actions.

4.4 An illustration

Let us consider an example that illustrates the development from biological determinism to moral behavior. The fight or flight response is biologically pre-wired in humans, as in other animals. The ability to recognize threatening behavior is apparently built up easily from pre-existing perceptual capacities.[42] Thus, a typical series of events can be represented by means of Figure 3.1 above, MacKay's simplest diagram. Let us say that it involves perception of the behavior of another person (R); evaluation of the behavior as threatening (C); selection of response – fleeing, fighting, conciliation – by the organizing system (O); and effecting the response (E). Feedback from the field of operation (F) will provide differential reinforcements that actually change the configuration of the brain.

This neurobiological change is an important factor for our enquiry here. Recall that our original worry was neurobiological determinism – that is, that the laws governing neural processes determine all of human thought and behavior. As already noted,

---

[41] MacIntyre, *Dependent Rational Animals*, 74–5.
[42] Brothers, *Friday's Footprint*, 25–30; cf. Thomas's *vis aestimativa*.

neural connections work on a "use it or lose it" principle. Much of the "wiring diagram" of the brain comes about through random growth of neurons and neural connections. Positive feedback makes connections stronger; absence of feedback or negative feedback weakens connections. This is the basis of habit and conditioning.

Let us suppose, then, that our agent has developed a habit of violent responses to threats. Jesuit priest and ethicist G. Simon Harak describes an event that exemplifies such conditioning:

> When I was younger, I studied karate for a few years, going three times a week for practice. One day, two fellow students of theology and I decided to go to a movie. Fran was a former Marine sergeant. John was a bright and articulate student. After we had bought our tickets individually, we regrouped in the lobby. "Did you see that guy on the other side of the ticket booth?" Fran asked me. "Yeah," I replied. "He sure was cruisin' for a bruisin', wasn't he?" "You know," Fran said, "the look on his face ... I was just waiting for him to try something," and he put his fist into his left palm. I started to say, "If he made a move on me, I would've. ..." But John interrupted us by saying, "What guy?"
>
> The facts are these: Fran and I saw this young man, and were ready even to fight with him. John, a bright and alert person, didn't even perceive him. Why? The key lies in our respective backgrounds. In our history, Fran and I shared a training in violence. It was, significantly, a *physical* training which *disposed* us to "take things in a certain way." Specifically, we were "looking for trouble." And we found it. John, with no such training, didn't even perceive the "belligerent" young man.[43]

MacIntyre's account of moral development involves self-transcendence – that is, becoming aware of and evaluating that which moves one to action. In Harak's case this evaluation happened as a result of the contrast between his and John's responses. He says: "I could see my deficiency precisely because of my association with

[43] G. Simon Harak, *Virtuous Passions* (New York: Paulist Press, 1993), 34.

John and others like him in another community."[44] The other community was the Jesuit order, and, in due course, he realized that he needed to give up his practice of martial arts, and adopted a pacifist ethic. This story fits MacIntyre's account of the emergence of moral responsibility. Harak became conscious of what moved him to action, and then evaluated it, first, in light of the norms of other community members, and finally in light of an abstract conception of the good.

To represent this process in information-engineering terms, we need the more complex diagram I presented as Figure 3.2. Notice that in Figure 3.1, I_g, the goal state of the system, is set by something outside the system – in the first instance it was set by natural selection. In Figure 3.2 the goal state itself is set by higher-level processes within the system. In the case of our pacifist, the meta-comparator places a higher value on nonviolent resolution of conflict than on survival. The meta-organizing system then adjusts C's priorities accordingly. C's job will now be to evaluate threatening behavior not in terms of threats to survival, but in terms of threats to the peace of the community. A different repertoire of skills and norms will have to be developed in O. As this system develops, the FF path, which selects relevant features of sensory input, will be affected by action and reactions of the environment. As Harak points out, virtuous behavior effects changes in the agent's perceptions.

Notice that in Figure 3.2 there is feedback from the field of operation to the meta-comparator. This represents the fact that, in the case in question, the moral principle is subject to readjustment in light of the effects produced by acting in accordance with it. For example, it is often supposed that pacifist responses increase others' aggression. The pacifist might re-evaluate his commitment to this principle if this turned out to be true.

So Figure 3.2 represents a system in which first the social environment and then an abstract moral concept exercise what we might call downward causal efficacy on an individual's behavior, and the change

[44] Ibid., 35.

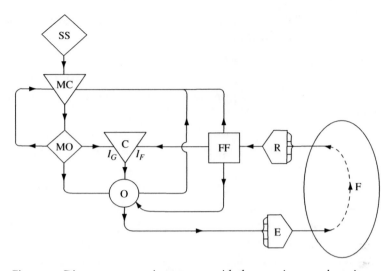

Figure 3.3. Diagram representing an agent with the capacity to evaluate its own prior evaluations.

in behavior will have an effect in reshaping neural connections in such a way that the new behavior becomes habitual. Thus we have a dynamic interplay between neurobiology and environment.

A worry arises, though, regarding the pacifist's moral responsibility: what if his acceptance of pacifism was *socially determined*, for example, because of a strong need for social conformity? Notice that if this worry occurs to Harak it provokes another level of self-transcendence. That is, it engages once again his ability to make himself the object of his reflections and evaluations. This means that as soon as the suspicion of social determination arises for the agent he is able to transcend that determination. In this case, he may invoke a higher-level evaluative principle to the effect that all genuine moral commitments must be accepted on the basis of autonomous rational examination, not on the authority of one's community. Representation of this second act of self-transcendence requires a more complex diagram (Figure 3.3)[45] in which a

---

[45] My modification of MacKay's figure.

higher-level supervisory system has been added that evaluates the meta-comparator of Figure 3.2.

In this figure the supervisory system, SS, represents the cognitive capacity to evaluate in light of a still more abstract goal the whole complex of motives and principles that, up until then, have moved him to act.

There is no limit, other than lack of imagination, to the ability of the agent to transcend earlier conceptions. For example, our pacifist may take a course in philosophical ethics and become persuaded that Alasdair MacIntyre's tradition-based approach to ethics is better argued than his previous Kantian position. He then comes to see his bid for moral autonomy as both unrealistic and culturally determined. So a higher level of meta-ethical evaluation overturns (or, alternatively, could have reinforced) his earlier ethical program. I shall claim in the next chapter that such a line of questioning will ultimately call for theological reflection.

5. But is this free will?

I began in the previous section with the question of why we want to argue for free will, and claimed that it is primarily for the sake of assigning moral responsibility. I pursued the question, then, of whether we could reconcile morally responsible action with what we know from the cognitive neurosciences. While we cannot yet give a detailed account in neurobiological terms, we saw that MacKay's account of complex self-directed systems gives us an idea of how an information processor with sophisticated language might be seen as acting in a morally responsible manner.

5.1 A confusion of definitions

But is this free will? A significant problem in answering this question is the fact that the very meaning of "free will" is highly contested among philosophers. In fact, even the preceding statement is highly contested. Philosophers of the ordinary-language variety claim that we know quite well enough what we mean when we say that someone did something freely: it means that one was able to act as one chose, and was not, for instance, compelled to do it by having a gun to one's head.

For other philosophers, the question is not merely whether one is able to act as one chooses, but whether one was able to *choose* freely. We can narrow down the problem to be addressed here by noting, only to set aside, a variety of supposed *threats* to the ability to choose freely. The oldest challenge to free will is fatalism, as in ancient Greek dramas. There are two versions of the problem arising from Christian theology – first, the claim that God's foreknowledge rules out human freedom, and second, a doctrine of predestination that denies human freedom with regard to matters of salvation. Yet another possibility is social determinism as in B. F. Skinner's theories of conditioning.

I set all of these problems aside, since the question at issue for the physicalist is neurobiological determinism. The worry is this: if human choices are essentially brain events, and if brain events are governed by the laws of neurobiology, then must it not be the case that all choices and all subsequent behavior are governed by the laws of neurobiology? The goal of the previous section was to show how a system with deterministic neurobiology could cease to be governed solely by the laws of neurobiology. We saw instead that interactions with the environment and higher-level evaluative processes alter neural structure. Thus, behavior is seldom controlled exclusively by neurobiology. More important here is the fact that our complex neurobiology enables us to conceive of abstract goals that become causal factors in their own right.

My plan in this final section is to survey accounts of free will in order to see whether any or all of them are satisfied by the pacifist described in the preceding section. I shall conclude that all but the most demanding versions of free will are satisfied, and that this most demanding version is not a coherent idea. I shall consider three conceptions of free will: the first is the concept, already mentioned, of free will as being able to act as one chooses. The second is the concept of free will as autonomy or as acting for a reason. The third is a concept of free will with a variety of names – libertarian, counterfactual, and incompatibilist free will.

Let us first consider free will as being able to act as one chooses. This concept is also sometimes called liberty of spontaneity or compatibilist free will, in the latter case because it is thought to be compatible with antecedent determination of actions, thoughts, and character. My examination of the complexities of human behavior, in contrast to that of machines and lower organisms, was precisely in order to lay out the factors that make humans and higher animals able to direct their behavior toward their own goals and to change those goals as appropriate. The sort of biological determinism that threatens such freedom is one in which we lack the ability to resist biological impulses or needs, as in the case of the chimpanzee that could not avoid choosing the larger pile of candy.

A second concept of free will, sometimes called autonomy, is the ability to subjugate one's behavior to the dictates of reason. This was addressed by considering the role of our linguistic abilities and the ability we have to evaluate and change our own cognitive processes.[46] Acting for a reason is often specified in terms of governing one's behavior according to reason in contrast to being overcome by emotions.[47] The point of considering the prerequisites for self-transcendence, that is, the ability to evaluate that which moves one to act, was precisely to see whether we could understand such

[46] For a more technical approach to reconciling reason and causation, see Nancey Murphy, "The Problem of Mental Causation: How Does Reason Get Its Grip on the Brain?" *Science and Christian Belief*, 14, no. 2 (October 2002): 143–58; and Murphy and Brown, *Did My Neurons Make Me Do It?*

[47] Damasio's work on the role of somatic markers – subtle emotional cues – in rational behavior provides empirical evidence that this disjunction of reason and emotion has been misguided. See Antonio Damasio, *Descartes' Error: Emotion, Reason and the Human Brain* (New York: G. P. Putnam's Sons, 1994).

a system in causal and information-processing terms. I claim that our pacifist satisfies this criterion as soon as his behavior changes in accordance with a moral principle. Many philosophers who argue for this concept of free will insist that an action cannot be simultaneously caused and undertaken for a reason. I hope to have shown, however, that there is no necessary opposition between reason and causation in the normal case.

Finally, we need to consider what I have called the most demanding concept of free will. This is the version that requires not only that one be able to act as one chooses, but that the choice itself not be causally determined. The criterion for such freedom is generally taken to be the ability to have chosen differently than one in fact did. Thus, the best name for this position is "counterfactual freedom." Other terms associated with this position in the literature are "libertarian free will," "liberty of indifference," and "incompatibilist free will." The latter term reflects the judgment that this sort of freedom is incompatible with causal determinism. I conclude, however, that the distinction between compatibilism and incompatibilism subtly misses the point.

5.2 A critique of the terms of debate

I noted at the beginning of section 4 my judgment that the current free-will debate is formulated in several unhelpful ways. The first of these is the distinction between "compatibilist" and "libertarian" accounts. The first question that is raised is whether free will is compatible with determinism. If one rejects the compatibilist view (e.g. that one is free if one can *act* as one chooses) then one has to ask what more is involved. The usual answer, as already noted, is the requirement that one be able to *choose* freely. But in order to choose freely, it must be the case that the choice was not itself caused by antecedent factors. If determinism is true, then there *must* have been a prior cause and so one was not free. So if one is not a compatibilist then one has to show that determinism is false in order to allow for "libertarian" free will.

I argue, however, that the compatibilist–incompatibilist debate is misguided, first, because the concept of determinism is so vague and, more importantly, it is beside the point. Before one can argue meaningfully that determinism rules out free will, one has to specify what is supposed to be determined *by what*. To be more precise, one has to ask what it is that is taken to determine human choices. I have set aside the ancient concept of fate, as well as the theological issues, because the goal here is defense of a physicalist anthropology, and these are no more of a problem for a physicalist than for a dualist. In B. F. Skinner's day social determinism was a pressing issue, but in our own day the threat of biological determinism – genetic or neurobiological – has displaced it.

Genetic determinism can be set aside for two reasons. First, instances of human behavior that are in any way candidates for free choice (unlike, for instance, height) are never perfectly correlated with genes. That is, identical twins show similarities in political attitudes, temperament, sexual orientation, and even religiosity, but the imperfect correlation means that genes are only part of the story. A second line of reasoning is based on the total quantity of information contained in the genome versus the total amount of information that would be needed to determine the synaptic connections in any particular individual's brain. The genes fall short of this capacity by several orders of magnitude.

In contrast to genetic determinism, I have taken the threat of neurobiological determinism to be real and highly significant. However, this more specific focus actually misses the point in a subtle way. The issue is not whether neurobiological processes are themselves determinate, but whether neurobiological *reductionism* is true. If I have made the case for the intelligibility of downward causation and its prevalence in shaping and reshaping the neural system, then the determinism of the laws of neurobiology is actually not relevant to the issue of free will. With an account of downward causation via selection, it makes no difference whether the laws of the bottom level are deterministic or not; higher-level selective processes can operate equally well on a range of possibilities that have been produced (at the lower level) by either random *or deterministic* processes.

In contrast to the atomist–reductionist assumption of the modern worldview, I have sketched a view of reality that recognizes the emergence, throughout cosmic history, of new and more complex entities, many of which possess new causal capacities. Some of these new capacities produce regular results, and thus their causal roles in the world can be modeled by deterministic laws. For example, the Hodgkin–Huxley laws that describe the transmission of nerve impulses are strict (deterministic) laws. If we give up the assumption that the behavior of all higher-level entities must be deterministic, and simply look, we see that there are also complex systems (e.g. organisms) that have emerged from (largely determinate) lower levels and that do not behave in regular (deterministic) ways. Much of this chapter has been taken up with a survey of the ways in which complex organisms become the *primary* causes of their own behavior.

My emphasis on the word "primary" in the preceding sentence leads to a critique of the second way in which the free will problem is badly framed. Free will is usually treated as an all-or-nothing affair; an act is or is not free. It is more helpful, I believe, to see human actions as *more or less* free. It is difficult to conceive of an action whose causal etiology involves *no* biological factors or social determinants. In fact, one should not want to act entirely independently of biology and social conditioning. Both our biology and our social institutions have developed in order to promote our survival and flourishing. The interesting question, then, comes closer to the kind of questions asked in a court of law: to what *extent* is this person responsible for her own act?

The behavior of infants is almost entirely determined by biology. The task of raising a toddler is that of replacing some natural biological tendencies with social controls. The maturation task is a process of reshaping the person's character so that she becomes increasingly the source of her own actions. This reshaping occurs, as MacIntyre points out, by means of a process of self-evaluation or self-transcendence. My recommendation is to say that when a person acts on the basis of considered goals and principles, without undue biological or social interference, she has become the author of her own acts and ought to be described as acting freely. This again, is free will understood as autonomy, but without the unrealistic expectation of total autonomy. If one wishes to withhold the term "free will" in such cases, then the dispute is merely a verbal disagreement.

In fact, the pursuit of total autonomy in the name of free will may be counterproductive. Consider again our pacifist. Let us return to the point at which he has been convinced by the teaching and example of the Jesuits to become a pacifist, but through an act of self-transcendence has come to suspect that his decision was determined by a need for social approval. The advocate of free will as autonomy might well raise the objection that surely something caused him to question the source of his pacifism, and if so, then again he is not free. To pursue this issue let us grant that there is a cause and let us further suppose that the causal factor is, in fact, his being given a book that convinces him of the ultimate importance of complete autonomy. Let us also suppose that this *causes* the emergence of a higher-level supervisory system which is *determined* to make freedom from biological and environmental determinism its highest priority. Detecting the influences of his community on the decision to become a pacifist, he immediately abandons his pacifism. But now he recognizes that he was caused to make this change by the book he was given, and so his highest-level supervisory system requires rejecting his rejection of pacifism. But acting contrarily to the authority of the book is to be equally influenced by the book, only in a negative way.

So what next? I think all we can predict is that the system will "go haywire" at this point. Donald MacKay used this term to describe what happens when a video camera is focused on its own monitor screen. If "we swing the camera to look at its own screen we find it is generating a pseudo picture. And if we zoom in to try to get more detail the whole thing goes haywire."[48] MacKay had other uses for the video analogy, but I propose it as an analogy for a system with the goal of attaining freedom understood as complete absence of biological and social causal factors. Here we have a system that at any moment can do otherwise than it is now doing. It can be a pacifist one moment and not the next. Another traditional name for this kind of freedom is liberty of indifference. We certainly have here a model of such freedom since all lower-level drives and goals, having been subordinated to the goal of freedom (so understood) are now irrelevant.

So I suggest that what we really want when we want free will is *some measure* of autonomy from biological drives and social forces. But not a *great* deal. After our vertiginous climb to a position transcending all causal factors, acting for a reason begins to look like a pretty good account of what we rational animals should want in the way of free will.

6. Retrospect

As noted above, physicalism has not been the predominant view of human nature in either Christian thought or the history of philosophy until quite recently. As a consequence there are a variety of philosophical issues that need to be addressed. The most serious, I claimed, is the threat of reductionism. If "*nonreductive* physicalism" is an oxymoron – if we are nothing but biological machines – then this is a position no Christian could accept. In fact, if reductionism were true, no rational person could accept it because there would be no rational persons!

---

[48] MacKay, op. cit., 10.

I have argued, instead, that our brain processes, suitably developed, enhanced by symbolic language, and engaged in social interaction provide us with capacities far greater than any of the animals' to direct our behavior in the pursuit of goals such as rationality, morality, and even freedom itself.

Thomas Aquinas defined the will as that faculty of the soul that enables us to be attracted to goods of a non-sensible nature. Since God is the ultimate good, the will is the faculty that provides for our attraction to God. In the next chapter we need to see if a physicalist can account for this ability as well.

4 | What are the philosophical challenges to physicalism? Human distinctiveness, divine action, and personal identity

1. Prospect

The goal of this chapter is to address a collection of philosophical problems facing the physicalist. Some of these are charges that any physicalist needs to be able to answer; others arise from specifically Christian concerns. The first is the simple (apparently simple?) question of how we know physicalism is true. The philosophical arguments seem to be interminable. I shall comment on the insufficiency of the sorts of arguments that are usually employed on behalf of dualism, and then sketch here my own proposal for the sort of argument that it would take to establish the truth of physicalism. I shall suggest that physicalism is best understood not as a philosophical thesis, but rather as the central component of a variety of well confirmed scientific theories.

Second, I shall deal with the problem of human distinctiveness: if we humans have no immortal souls to distinguish us from animals, then what is it that gives us a special place in God's creation? My answer will be that our distinctiveness lies primarily in the fact that we are able to be addressed by God and heed God's calling and commands. This will call for an examination of the issues of morality and religious experience. The topic of religious experience raises another issue. For humans to have experience of God, they must be capable of being affected by God in some way. Traditional views have taken the soul to be the "site" of divine action in human life. I argue instead that God relates to us through our *bodily* capacities. Thus, I shall address a third problem, the problem of how God acts in the physical world.

Finally, I shall consider the problem of personal identity. Many dualists object that if there is no soul then there is no way to account for how I can be the same person now as when I was much younger, or worse, how I could be the same person after the resurrection, with a very different body. This leads to a consideration of what we can and cannot know about the transformation that awaits us at the end.

2. The epistemological issue

Philosophical arguments for dualism and against dualism, for physicalism and against. How is the issue to be resolved? I mentioned above that recent successes of the cognitive neurosciences in studying mental capacities as brain functions have provided strong motivation for physicalism. However, science can never *prove* that there is no soul, a soul whose capacities are simply well *correlated* with brain functions. But can philosophical arguments prove that dualism is true? I shall not attempt here a thorough survey of dualist arguments, but shall rather comment on an approach to philosophical method shared by many such arguments, and explain why I find the arguments unconvincing.

2.1 On the unreliability of philosophical intuitions

Richard Swinburne is probably the most influential dualist philosopher.[1] Swinburne's argument for dualism depends on the fact that he can *conceive* of his body dying one night and his continuing to exist the next day. This reliance on conceivable situations and what they imply is typical of many dualist arguments. It is an approach to philosophy that owes its origin to René Descartes (1596–1650), considered the founder of modern philosophy. I shall attempt to explain why I see such arguments as unreliable.

[1] Richard Swinburne, *The Evolution of the Soul*, revised ed. (Oxford: Clarendon, 1997).

Descartes is famous for having set out to doubt everything that he had learned from the philosophical tradition in order to place knowledge on a new and certain foundation. He believed that if everyone followed his method, all would come to the same conclusions. He began with introspection, asking what ideas he could find in his mind that he was unable to doubt. His criterion was that any idea that appeared clearly and distinctly to him must be true.

The problem many have noted with Descartes's method is that what appears clear and distinct to one person sometimes turns out not to be so to others. For example, a "clear and distinct" premise of one of his arguments for the existence of God is that "it is manifest by the natural light that there must be at least as much reality in the efficient and total cause as in its effect ..."[2] This idea is not at all clear and distinct to people today; in fact it is so unclear that we might want to say that it is neither true nor false.

Another example of such conflicting philosophical intuitions appears in the philosophical arguments for and against dualism. For example, Stuart Goetz bases his argument for dualism on the intuition that he is a soul, distinct from his body. Yet in the same essay Goetz reports Peter van Inwagen's contrary intuition: "When I enter most deeply into that which I call *myself*, I *seem* to discover that I am a living animal."[3]

Many philosophers have concluded that such intuitions are unreliable grounds for philosophy simply because of such conflicts. In addition, they believe it is possible to explain the source of (many) such intuitions. Wallace Matson says that the thing Descartes failed to doubt was his own language – not his Latin or French (whatever that could mean) – but rather what twentieth-century philosopher

---

[2] René Descartes, *Meditations on First Philosophy*, third meditation; *Meditations and Other Metaphysical Writings*, trans. Desmond M. Clarke (London: Penguin, 2003), 35.

[3] Stuart Goetz, "Substance Dualism," in Joel B. Green and Stuart L. Palmer, eds., *In Search of the Soul: Four Views of the Mind-Body Problem* (Downers Grove, MI: InterVarsity, 2005), 55; quoting Peter van Inwagen, "Dualism and Materialism: Athens and Jerusalem?" *Faith and Philosophy* 12 (1995): 476.

Ludwig Wittgenstein would call the *grammar* of his language. "Grammar" in this special sense refers to the implicit rules for the use of central concepts. The "grammar" of scholastic language allowed for using the word "real" in a comparative manner, whereas ours allows us to say only that something is real or unreal. This accounts for the fact that Descartes's intuition was clear and distinct to him, while it makes no sense to us.[4]

An interesting fact about contemporary culture is that we have competing systems of language available for talking about ourselves. We still have the traditional language of bodies and souls (as my quiz in chapter 1 demonstrates), which allows us to say, for instance, that "when my body dies I shall be with God." However, new ways of talking have been developing for some years now.

If our most basic intuitions about ourselves are dependent on the kind of language we have learned, this seems to call for ways to evaluate the language itself. One way is to examine the sources of the different linguistic systems. If, as I have shown, recent scientific theories are a major source of the new physicalist language, where did the dualist language come from? I believe that it, too, comes from theories – theories developed in the distant past. One suggestion is that dualist theories were devised for ethical reasons: it is clear that people do not receive just rewards and punishments in this life. Thus, it was hypothesized that there must be another life apart from the body in which justice is done. For some Greek philosophers, as already noted, the concept of the soul served various explanatory purposes, such as to account for the differences between living and non-living things. Even Augustine accepted dualism partly for its explanatory value. He did not believe that there could be a physical account of memory:

> What this power is and whence it comes I think can be understood. It is certainly not from the heart or blood or brain, nor out of atoms . . .

[4] Wallace I. Matson, *A New History of Philosophy*, 2 vols. (San Diego: Harcourt Brace Jovanovich, 1987), 2:276–80.

I ask you, does it really seem to you that so great a power as memory could be congealed from earth and its dark cloudy sky?[5]

The important question for philosophy, then, is the source of the linguistic resources, and whether those habitual or newly minted forms of language are congruent with the way things really are. This requires, in turn, that one ask whether the theories of, say, Plato or Aristotle are better supported than contemporary neuroscientific theories about the sources of our capacities for cognition, emotion, and all of the other faculties that earlier theorists had attributed to the soul or mind.

2.2 Physicalism as a scientific research program

I have argued (elsewhere) that the best way to view the contest between dualism and physicalism is to treat each position not merely as a philosophical thesis but as the "hard core" of a scientific research program.[6] This argument is based on the philosophy of science of Imre Lakatos, who argued that research programs in science are unified by metaphysical theses about the essential nature of the subject-matter under investigation. So, for example, atomism is the philosophical thesis behind modern physics and chemistry.[7] In this light, it is clear that the physicalist program is doing extremely well: all recent advances in neurobiological understanding of cognition, emotion, and action, as well as progress in certain forms of cognitive science, are the product of a physicalist understanding of

---

[5] Augustine, *Tusc.* 1:60–1; quoted and translated by Phillip Carey, *Augustine's Invention of the Inner Self: The Legacy of a Christian Platonist* (Oxford: Oxford University Press, 2000), 134.

[6] See my "Nonreductive Physicalism: Philosophical Issues," in Brown, *et al.*, eds., *Whatever Happened to the Soul?*, 127–48; esp. 139–42.

[7] Imre Lakatos, "Falsification and the Methodology of Scientific Research Programmes," in *The Methodology of Scientific Research Programmes: Philosophical Papers, Volume 1*, ed. John Worrall and Gregory Currie (Cambridge: Cambridge University Press, 1978), 8–101.

human nature. In contrast, scarcely any research follows from a dualist theory; Sir John Eccles has been the only noted scientist whose research was based on body–mind dualism. He believed that the mind could influence physical processes at the quantum level in the brain and so solve the mind-brain interaction problem. Nothing, finally, has come of his project. Thus, however inconclusive the philosophical arguments may be, we can say that *science* provides as much evidence as could be desired for the physicalist thesis.

3. Human distinctiveness

I noted in chapter 2 that many have objected to evolutionary theory on the grounds that it shows us to be closely related to the animals. These same objections are raised against physicalists. In fact, some philosophers would say that a better term for the physicalist's position would be "animalism" – humans are nothing but animals. This is, of course, another way of raising the challenge to distinguish between reductive and nonreductive physicalism. The nonreductive physicalist says that the difference between humans and (other) animals is not found in a special immortal part, but rather in special capabilities, enabled by our more complex neural systems, language, and culture.

I also mentioned in chapter 2 that Pope Pius XII was one of many thinkers who resolved apparent conflicts between evolutionary theory and Christian teaching by invoking the special creation of the human soul at conception. He used this account to delimit the scope of science's investigation of human origins. More recently Pope John Paul II made a statement that bears on these issues.[8]

---

[8] Pope John Paul II, "Message to the Pontifical Academy of Sciences" (22 October, 1996), *L'Osservatore Romano*, 44 (October 30, 1996); reprinted in Robert Russell *et al.*, eds., *Evolutionary and Molecular Biology: Scientific Perspectives on Divine Action* (Vatican City State and Berkeley, CA: Vatican Observatory and Center for Theology and the Natural Sciences, 1998), 2–9.

Addressing a plenary session of the Pontifical Academy of Sciences, he reaffirmed the teaching of Pius XII regarding the compatibility of evolutionary biology with Catholic teaching, so long as certain qualifications are borne in mind. One of these qualifications concerns human origins. John Paul quoted Pius's statement that "if the human body takes its origin from pre-existent living matter, the spiritual soul is immediately created by God."[9] Many readers take Pope John Paul to be affirming the same dualist anthropology and the same limits to the scientific study of humankind. However, as George Coyne, director of the Vatican Observatory, points out, after the quotation from Pius XII, the word "soul" does not reappear in the document.[10] Rather than speak of the moment when the soul is created, John Paul II speaks of "the moment of transition to the spiritual."[11] Science cannot determine this point, he says, but it can determine at the experimental level a series of signs indicating what is specific to the human being. In addition, philosophical analysis can reflect on what is distinctively human. The Pope lists metaphysical knowledge, self-awareness and self-reflection, moral conscience, freedom, aesthetic experience, and religious experience. But only theology, he says, can bring out the ultimate meaning of these characteristics according to the Creator's plans.

What, then, does it mean to reflect *scientifically* on the question of human distinctiveness? A number of scientists study the higher primates and from these studies one could construct a list of capacities typical of humans that are not shared by the (other) animals. As it turns out, most of the differences are matters of degree rather than of the presence and total absence of certain characteristics. However, small differences in basic capacities interact to produce huge differences in final outcome. For example,

---

[9] Quoted in John Paul II, "Message," 6.

[10] George V. Coyne, S. J., "Evolution and the Human Person: The Pope in Dialogue," in Russell *et al.*, eds., *Evolutionary and Molecular Biology*, 11–17.

[11] Pope John Paul II, "Message," 6.

chimpanzees can be taught rudimentary forms of language. There is debate over the question of whether chimpanzees also possess self-awareness (one of the distinctive features listed by the Pope). Do chimpanzees recognize themselves in a mirror? Perhaps it depends on what we mean: chimpanzees do *recognize* themselves, but do they recognize them*selves*? That is, they do not have a symbolic self-*concept*. Higher animals have emotions, but ours are more finely modulated. Animals can be angry, but cannot experience righteous indignation. We saw in chapter 2 that some animals exhibit the sort of caring for one another that we prize for moral reasons.

Now, what does theology have to say about human distinctiveness? Here the question is not so much what it is that makes us different from animals, although differences have to be presupposed. Here the question is rather: what is it about us that is important to God? I shall emphasize two factors: the first is our capacity for morality, already addressed in the previous chapter; the second is our capacity for relationships, with God as well as with other humans. This emphasis on proper relationships is what is central to New Testament teaching on what it means to be human.

The point I emphasize here is that scientific results do not interpret themselves. That is, in addition to all that science can tell us about ourselves, we need a religious point of view in order to know the significance of the scientific findings. This is what I take Pope John Paul to mean when he says that only theology can bring out the ultimate meaning of these characteristics according to the Creator's plans.

3.1 Morality versus animal altruism

Morality has become a hot topic for debate among evolutionary psychologists. Some claim that genetics can explain human morality, and the arguments go something like this. Human morality has parallels in the animal world and even among insects. The parallel is that they all exhibit altruism, meaning that the individual sacrifices itself for the good of the group. This can be explained in animal behavior because group survival is generally survival of kin, and kinship survival means survival of one's genes. Evolution favors whatever is good for the survival of one's genes. Hence, human morality can be seen, also, as a product of genetics.

Recent arguments are much more nuanced than this but, however sophisticated, there is something wrong at the core of such an account. First a philosophical analysis. One of the most prominent philosophers of the modern period was Immanuel Kant. According to Kant, to be moral is to do one's duty. This means that if you do only what you are genetically programmed to do, or even act on what you are predisposed to find enjoyable, the action does not count as moral behavior at all. Being moral is not just doing good, it involves, essentially, doing good for the right motive. Kant's particular view is that the right motive has to be that you recognize it as a duty. Already we see an essential difference between what a human is doing when engaging in a moral action and anything an animal or insect could be doing. We saw (in chapter 3) MacIntyre's claim that moral responsibility does not appear until children attain the ability to evaluate their own motives, desires, reasons.

Now let us move to a theological level of analysis. We can ask the further question: where do moral duties come from? The traditional theological answer is that duties come from God. That is, morality for Christians and for those in the other monotheistic traditions is, at its heart, obedience. Kant tried to show that we could know our duty on the basis of pure reason, but at the end of this modern Enlightenment experiment there is an increasing number of philosophers who believe that moral reasoning finally calls for some answer to the question of the nature of ultimate reality.[12]

---

[12] See, for example, Alasdair MacIntyre, *After Virtue*, 2nd edn. (Notre Dame: University of Notre Dame Press, 1984); and Bernard Williams, *Morality: An Introduction to Ethics* (Cambridge: Cambridge University Press, 1972).

So here we take a further step away from equating human morality with animal altruism. The theological interpretation of morality is theocentric. One does what one does because it is obligatory, and it is obligatory because it fits with God's purposes for human life. To sacrifice oneself for others, on this account, is as different as it could possibly be from doing it because it is genetically programmed.

Let us consider the content of morality as well as its motive. On the surface it may appear that the sociobiologist has it just right: self-sacrifice is central to Christian morality. But let us look more closely. The sociobiologists' account depends on similarity of genes in the group for which one sacrifices; that is, they must be family, kin. Christian morality is in some ways strangely anti-family. Jesus says: I have come to set a man against his father, and a daughter against her mother ... and one's foes will be members of one's own household (Mt. 10:35–6).

The emphasis in Christianity is rather on loving the stranger (and this is a part of Jewish morality as well). For Christians the one for whom one is to sacrifice is, most particularly, the enemy. Later New Testament teaching focused on reconciliation of Jews and Gentiles, whom no one at the time could have considered to be physically related. So Christian morality is different not only in motive but in content from kin-preserving altruism.

Thus, I maintain that science studies the whole of human life – there is no metaphysically distinct part of us that is immune from scientific investigation. However, science gives us an incomplete account of human life, an account that can only be put into perspective by a religious point of view. Science can say: in this, this, and this way we humans are like the animals, and in that way and that way we are different. But then the question is: so what? Birds sacrifice themselves for the group; humans sacrifice themselves for the group. Which similarities matter and why? Which differences matter, and why? Only a worldview that address ultimate issues can answer this question.

This is one way of distinguishing between reductionist and non-reductionist accounts of the human person. Reductive physicalism says that humans are physical organisms, and nothing but that, and in addition – and this is the reductionistic part – *everything* about us can be explained in naturalistic terms. Nonreductive physicalism, on the other hand, grants that we are biological organisms, but emphasizes that our neurobiological complexity and the history of cultural development have together resulted in the capacity for genuine moral reasoning.

3.2 Physicalism and religious experience

I come now to a second and closely related point of human distinctiveness, the ability to be in relationship with God. The ability to have religious experience has often been thought to be dependent on the soul. Medieval mystics spoke of withdrawing from the world of the senses, entering into the soul, wherein they experienced God's presence. How could one conceive of experiencing God if there is no soul?

Philosopher Nicholas Wolterstorff provides an account of experiencing God, in fact an account of hearing God speak, in his book titled *Divine Discourse*. Wolterstorff says:

> Let me present part of the narration of some experiences which recently befell an acquaintance of mine who is a well-established member of the faculty of one of the old, Eastern seaboard universities . . . I shall call her "Virginia" . . . and call [her pastor] "Byron." Perhaps I should add that though Virginia is . . . a Christian, she neither is nor was what anyone would classify as an *Evangelical*. It's worth saying that because Evangelicals have the reputation of believing that God speaks to them rather more often, and rather more trivially, than most of us think God would bother with.

Here is Virginia's own account:

> On February 12, 1987, while folding laundry I suddenly knew with certain knowledge that Byron was supposed to leave St. Paul's

Church. There was no external voice, but there was a brightening in the room at the moment of revelation. The experience was so overwhelming that I called my husband and invited him to come home for lunch . . . I needed to reassure myself of reality. Later that afternoon . . . I found myself sobbing. I knew the knowledge I have been given was not me, and I knew it was correct. As the day progressed, it became clear to me that there were seven insistent statements that I needed to tell Byron . . . I was awe-struck and terrified . . .

The next morning, when I went to see Byron . . . I told him the seven statements: "Your work is done here. You have accomplished what you were sent to do. You are still young. There are great things in store for you. Do not be afraid. God will take care of you. I will help with the transition." This message was not a surprise to Byron. He had already come to that conclusion prior to our conversation.[13]

Virginia goes on to tell about the ways in which her message was confirmed in the days to come. There was a second message to be delivered to a meeting at church, which was well-received as just the thing that needed saying. Byron did get a call to another church. In addition, Virginia's own spirituality deepened.

Notice how ordinary this experience was – not ordinary in the sense that people regularly report getting messages from God, but in the sense that it used or depended on nothing but ordinary cognitive abilities that we all have. A set of *ideas* came into her mind. She had a variety of *feelings* – a feeling of certitude, a feeling of awe. I submit that for such an experience, nothing is needed on our part beyond the ordinary neural equipment that we all possess. Because of the ordinariness, I doubt that brain scans will show there to be any particular location peculiar to religious experience.[14]

[13] Nicholas Wolterstorff, *Divine Discourse: Philosophical Reflections on the Claim that God Speaks* (Cambridge: Cambridge University Press, 1995), 274–5.

[14] See my "Nonreductive Physicalism," in Brown, *et al.*, eds., *Whatever Happened to the Soul*, for a typology of religious experience and an argument that all of these kinds of experience can be understood as *mediated* by ordinary cognitive and affective capacities.

What makes this a religious experience is that it was attributed to God. The question is, then, if it was so ordinary (in the sense I have specified), how could one *know* it was from God? Wolterstorff takes up this question, pointing out that the circumstances in which it happened, the consequences, and the confirmation by the community all pointed in that direction. I would add that this sort of judgment reflects quite well the regular criteria that Christians have used all along in practices of individual and communal discernment to distinguish between their own fancies and the voice of God.[15]

So I have mentioned a variety of features that are associated with our sense of what it means to be human, and animals share rudimentary forms of most of them. What matters is the way these enhanced capacities interact in human life. For example, put together our clear sense of self with finely tuned emotions and subtle linguistic abilities and we have immensely different capacities for interpersonal relationships, including the capacity to recognize and obey the voice of God.[16]

4. Divine action in the natural world

I have just addressed briefly the question of what it takes, on a physicalist account, for humans to be able to relate to God. A correlative question is what it takes for God to be able to relate to us. Given the long-held assumption that God interacts with souls, how can God communicate with us if we have no such thing? This is a serious problem but, I argue, not for the reason many assume.

---

[15] See Nancey Murphy, *Theology in the Age of Scientific Reasoning* (Ithaca, NY: Cornell University Press, 1990), chapter 5, for criteria from a number of Christian traditions for judging the authenticity of religious experience.

[16] See Warren S. Brown, "Cognitive Contributions to Soul," in Brown, *et al.*, eds., *Whatever Happened to the Soul?* chapter 5.

4.1 Why this should not be a problem

The physicalist says that if it is our bodies that perform all of the functions once attributed to the soul, then God must have to do with bodies, particularly our neural systems. I find that there is a great deal of resistance to this proposal. We have certainly seen a variety of reasons why Christians have found it natural to believe that souls are the means by which God relates to us. There was Augustine's roomy chamber of memory into which one may enter and find God. There was the medieval cosmic picture in which God directed earthly processes via angels and the *seven* planets, but engaged human souls through the Church's *seven* sacraments.

Nonetheless, Christians have regularly taught that God is not only beyond the cosmos (transcendent) but also immanent in *all* of creation, including the physical, acting at least to sustain its existence and often to govern its processes. Most Christians, along with their biblical predecessors, have believed that God also acts in special ways, in signs or miracles, to save and guide, and that these special events often involve changes in physical objects. Why, then, the resistance to assuming that God makes us aware of the divine presence, speaks to us, heals our emotions, by acting on the neural and other bodily processes that give rise to consciousness?

I speculate here. I believe that contemporary Christians are still prey to *attitudes* that developed in the ancient and medieval periods under the influence of the idea of the great chain of being. I have already suggested that this world picture helps to account for our reluctance to be compared with animals (chapter 2, section 3.1). Recall that the great ontological divide, on this account, is between matter and spirit. Human souls were above the divide, bodies below. Philosopher Daniel Dennett has, perhaps, put his finger on the issue in language a theologian would be reluctant to use: "One widespread tradition has it that we humans beings are responsible agents, captains of our fate, *because* we really are *souls*, immaterial and immortal clumps of Godstuff that inhabit and control our material bodies rather like spectral puppeteers. It is our souls that are the source of all meaning, and the locus of all our suffering, our joy, our glory and shame."[17] While Christian teaching vehemently denies that souls are "Godstuff," there seems to be an unspoken assumption that God can only communicate with something closely akin, in a metaphysical sense, to God's own substance. This is what many take it to mean when Genesis 1:27 says that we are created in the image of God.

Theologian James McClendon laments our modern-day alienation from biblical ways of thought, particularly alienation from the Bible's appreciation of our own embodied selfhood. This has been accompanied by a denigration of the organic and natural world of which we are a part. He describes our difficulty in this way: "We simply do not believe that the God we know will have to do with *things*."[18] So Bible-readers should not fear that the God we know will have nothing to do with *bodies*.

Nonetheless, thanks to scientific and philosophical changes, beginning with the modern revolution in physics, God's action in the physical world has become a serious philosophical and theological problem.

4.2 The modern challenge

In the medieval period, as just noted, God's action in the world could be explained in a way perfectly consistent with the scientific knowledge of the time. But modern science has changed all that, primarily by its dependence on the concept of *the laws of nature*. The notion of a law of nature began as a metaphorical extension of the idea of a divinely sanctioned moral code. For early modern scientists, as well as for medieval theologians, the laws of nature provided an account of how God managed the physical universe. In fact, Descartes took the

---

[17] Daniel C. Dennett, *Freedom Evolves* (New York: Viking, 2003), 1.

[18] James W. McClendon, Jr., *Ethics: Systematic Theology, Volume 1*, 1st edn. (Nashville, TN: Abingdon Press, 1984), 90–1.

laws of motion to follow from a more basic principle, explicitly theological: "God is the First Cause of movement and ... always preserves an equal amount of movement in the universe."[19]

However, after a century or so the metaphorical character of the term "law of nature" had been forgotten. The laws were granted some form of real existence independent of God, and it is one of the ironies of history that later they even came to be seen as *obstacles* to divine purposes. Whereas, for Isaac Newton (1642–1727), a complete account of the motions of the solar system had required both the divinely willed laws of motion and God's constant readjustment, for his successor Pierre Simon de Laplace (1749–1827) it was no longer necessary for God to make adjustments and, finally, the question was raised whether it was even *conceivable* that God should intervene. First, if God acts, this requires that God violate, over-ride, or suspend the laws of nature, which otherwise would have brought about some different event. Many have argued that this is an unacceptable view of the nature of God. If God created the laws in the first place, then God's violation of them is irrational; the Jewish philosopher Baruch Spinoza (1632–77) argued that in such a case God would be involved in self-contradiction. Second, if action in the material world requires a force, then to conceive of God making things happen in the world is to conceive of God as a force among forces. This, too, is theologically problematic, since it reduces God to the level of a Demiurge.

The simplest reconciliation of divine action with the modern conception of the clockwork universe was Deism, a very popular option in the eighteenth century. The Deists, whose number in America included Thomas Jefferson and Benjamin Franklin, concluded that while God was the creator of the universe and author of the laws of nature, God was not at all involved in ongoing natural processes or in human affairs. They maintained a notion of God as the source of moral principles, but the most extreme rejected all the rest of positive religion, including the notion of revelation.

[19] René Descartes, *Principles of Philosophy* (1644), part II, xxxvi.

I have argued (elsewhere) that for those who would stay within the Christian fold, there have been but two options, here labeled "interventionism" and "immanentism."[20] Interventionism has generally been the doctrine of choice for conservative theologians. These theologians hold that in addition to God's creative activity, which includes ordaining the laws of nature, God occasionally violates or suspends those very laws in order to bring about an extraordinary event. God makes something happen that would not have happened in the ordinary course of nature. Note that the assumption held by some contemporary Christians that an event is an act of God only if it cannot be explained by natural laws is, on this account, a degenerate view of divine action. God works in the regular processes just as much as in miraculous interventions. Much of the controversy over evolution would dissolve if it were not assumed by many conservatives that scientific accounts and accounts of divine creative action are mutually exclusive.

The immanentist view of divine action, developed by nineteenth-century liberal protestants, was a reaction both against Deism, with its view that God is not active at all within the created world, and against the conservative theologians' view that God performs special, miraculous acts. The liberal view emphasizes the universal presence of God in the world, and God's continual, creative, and purposive activity in and through all the processes of nature and history. This view made it possible to understand progress, both evolutionary progress in the natural world and human progress in society, as manifestations of God's purposes.

A primary motive for emphasizing God's action *within* natural processes was the acceptance of the modern scientific view of the world as a closed system of natural causes, along with the judgment

---

[20] See Nancey Murphy, *Beyond Liberalism and Fundamentalism: How Modern and Postmodern Philosophy Set the Theological Agenda* (Valley Forge, PA: Trinity Press International, 1996), chapter 3. I believe that this disjunctive account of divine action has been the most important factor dividing liberal and conservative Protestants in the modern era.

that a view of divine activity as intervention reflected an inferior grasp of God's intelligence and power. That is, it suggested that God was unable to achieve all of the divine purposes though an original ordering, and also that God was inconsistent in willing laws and then also willing their violation. In short, the higher view of divine action was thought to be one in which God did not need to intervene. Thus, the interpretation of divine activity in terms of miracles tended to disappear in the liberal tradition. The conservative response to this position is simply to note that it requires one to give up too much of traditional Christian teaching. My criticism is that it makes God's action something of a "rubber stamp" approval of the natural course of events.

It is worth noting that this same view of nature as a closed causal order was an important motivation for dualism. The body may be determined by Newton's laws, but the soul is free. This of course only pushed the problem back one step: how can the soul or mind "intervene" in the natural order that is its body?

4.3 Current proposals

It is appropriate, given that early modern science and associated philosophical moves created the problem of divine action, to ask what difference recent developments in both of these fields might make. Notice that two quite different (though related) problems confronted modern attempts to give an account of divine action. One was the assumption that God would have to violate or suspend the laws of nature to bring about any *special* divine act (recall that both liberals and conservatives supposed that God acted constantly through the laws of nature). The other problem was the question of how God could act in a universe where all causes were believed ultimately to be physical forces if God was not a physical force. Newtonian physics was believed to account for all natural forces as purely mechanical in character.

The short answer to the problem of divine action is the following: the first problem was created by the *mistaken* assumption that all causation was bottom-up. Now, as I have argued in the previous chapter, we recognize as well top-down causation and genuinely new causal factors at higher levels of the hierarchy of the sciences.[21] These higher-level factors need to be consistent with the lower-level laws, but their effects cannot be reduced to them. So it was simply a mistake to suppose that the laws of physics determine all natural events. The second problem was created by the atomist picture of matter and by an overemphasis on mechanical causes. Science itself has moved far beyond this conception of natural causation, so the old arguments based on such a picture should no longer stand in the way of belief in special divine acts.

Is the short answer adequate? We can certainly make the following negative statement: in light of these two sorts of changes – the non-reductionist conception of the hierarchy of the sciences and the changes in physics since Newton's day – it is no longer the case that we have clear scientific reasons for rejecting claims regarding special divine actions. In a sense this puts us back to square one: as in the early and middle centuries of Christianity, we have no good reasons (philosophical or scientific) to deny special divine actions, and, I would claim, much theological reason to affirm them.

However, we still need to recognize the intrinsic difference between the kinds of action available to physical entities (however much richer today's conception of physical agents may be) and the specific character of divine acts. It is to be expected that God's mode of action will be appropriate to the kind of agent that God is. This was the point of the medieval distinction between primary and secondary causation, and continues to be upheld in most theological accounts. The critical issue is to avoid reducing God to a mere physical cause, yet to find ways of recognizing that God's intentional action can bring about events above and beyond what could be accomplished merely by holding natural processes and causes in existence.

---

[21] Note that this is not to say that there are any new causal forces in addition to those known to physics.

In the medieval period it was possible to give an intelligible account in terms of then current science and philosophy of how conceptions of divine action and natural causation could be *integrated*. Some theologians and philosophers believe that such an integrative account should be attempted in our own day, using current science.[22] Among those who seek to integrate scientific and theological accounts of causation there are two prominent strategies. One is Arthur Peacocke's claim that God works solely in a top-down manner, influencing the whole of the universe in a way analogous to the environment's influence on an organism, or the whole person's influence on his or her own bodily actions.[23] The difficulty with this latter analogy is that it suggests either that God is like the mind or soul of the universe (a dualism that Peacocke rejects), or else a pantheistic view of God and the world – that is, an identification of God and the universe. Apart from either of these moves, Peacocke's metaphors or analogies have to be understood merely as metaphors. Furthermore, I have endorsed an account of downward causation in terms of *selection* among lower-level causal processes. So, on this account Peacocke would need to answer the question of *how* God acts so as to select one earthly process over another, and this is just to restate the question of how God exercises causal influence in the world. Nonetheless, the concept of top-down causation, with its recognition of the reality of higher-level entities, and the necessity of acknowledging them to be genuine causal agents, clears away many obstacles to an account of divine action.

---

[22] The Vatican Observatory, at the request of Pope John Paul II, has sponsored a series of six conferences on divine action in light of current developments in science. All of the books mentioned in this volume edited by Robert J. Russell are products of that series.

[23] See Arthur Peacocke, "God's Interaction with the World: The Implications of Deterministic 'Chaos' and of Interconnected and Interdependent Complexity," in Robert J. Russell, Nancey Murphy, and Arthur Peacocke, eds., *Chaos and Complexity: Scientific Perspectives on Divine Action* (Vatican City State and Berkeley, CA: Vatican Observatory and Center for Theology and the Natural Sciences, 1995), 263–88.

The second strategy for giving an account of the locus of divine action explores quantum physics and seeks to give an account of God's action throughout the natural and human world by means of action at the quantum level (either alone or in conjunction with top-down action). My own proposal is motivated theologically. If God is immanent in and acting in *all* creatures, then necessarily God is acting at the quantum level. Emphasis on this fact has the advantage of sidestepping the problem of interventionism: the laws of quantum mechanics are only statistical and therefore not subject to violation. If, as most interpreters conclude, events at this level are genuinely indeterminate, then there need be no competition between divine action and physical causation. It is possible from a theistic perspective to interpret current physics as saying that the natural world is intrinsically incomplete and open to divine action at its most basic level.[24]

There are vociferous debates about the cogency of accounts of this sort, many due to continuing debates about quantum physics itself.[25] Many of the criticisms have to do with the claim that God's action at the quantum level would have too few meaningful effects at the macroscopic level. These critics often assume (for unstated reasons) that such macro-level effects would have to be the result of God's determining the outcome of a single quantum event. I argue that if God's action is located at the quantum level then the scope of God's control would indeed be limited (to an extent we cannot determine without better understanding of the relations between quantum physics and the rest of science). However, this is not a

---

[24] See my "Divine Action in the Natural Order: Buridan's Ass and Schrödinger's Cat," in Robert Russell *et al.*, eds., *Chaos and Complexity*, 325–57.

[25] For a sample of the literature, see Robert Russell, ed., *Chaos and Complexity*; Robert Russell *et al.*, eds., *Quantum Mechanics: Scientific Perspectives on Divine Action* (Vatican City State and Berkeley, CA: Vatican Observatory and Center for Theology and the Natural Sciences, 2001). A volume evaluating the entire series of divine action conferences is projected for the future.

defect in a theory of divine action but rather an asset because it helps to explain why a benevolent God does not act more frequently and dramatically to remedy the sufferings of humans and other sentient creatures. Perhaps it will turn out that this attempt to integrate divine action and natural causation will explain the fact that the vast majority of Christians expect and pray for some sorts of divine assistance (healing, good weather, and especially our personal relationships with God) but not others (filling teeth, restoring lost limbs).

But however the arguments turn out regarding any specific proposal of this sort, the very existence of this growing body of literature should reassure us of the conceivability of God's action in the physical world, and especially of God's action in our own lives *and bodies*.

5. Personal identity

Another problem for the physicalist is that of personal identity. The term "identity" is used in reference to persons in several ways. The sense that is *not* at issue in this essay is the psychological sense in which people are said to seek, or lose, or regain their identities. In philosophical literature, numerical identity is distinguished from qualitative identity. It is the former that is at issue here: what are the criteria by which I am the same person now as I was forty years ago, even though qualitatively I am quite different?

Dualists have assumed that it is the soul that accounts for identity through time; reductive physicalists would seem to have to say that it is the body, however much it may change. I shall here attempt to sketch a nonreductive physicalist account. It is not the body *qua* material object that constitutes our identities, but rather the higher capacities that it enables: consciousness and memory, moral character, interpersonal relations, and, especially, relationship with God.

5.1 Philosophical distinctions

There is a rich philosophical literature on personal identity, in the sense of re-identification of persons after a lapse of time. Unfortunately many theological discussions of pre- and post-resurrection identity overlook some of the most important contributions. First, David Wiggins has shown that to say "x is the same as y" or "x is identical to y" requires the specification of a *covering concept*; one needs to be able to answer the question: "the same *what* as y?" This solves many traditional philosophical puzzles such as whether or not one can step into the same river twice. Criteria of identity need to be tailored to fit the relevant covering concept.[26] Consequently, in discussing personal identity it is necessary to ask specifically what are the identity criteria for the covering concept *person*, and to expect that these be different from identity criteria for a material object or even for a human body.[27] The classic work on the concept of *person* is P. F. Strawson's *Individuals*. Strawson argues that the concept *person* is a primitive concept applying to entities to which both states of consciousness and corporeal characteristics can be attributed.[28] The concept of mental life derives from the concept of person, not the other way around.

On the basis of evidence from both neurobiology and neurology, Leslie Brothers argues that the person concept is not merely an artifact of culture; we are biologically prepared to subscribe to the concept just as we are biologically prepared to learn language. Just as we are unable to hear a word in a familiar language without perceiving the meaning, our brains have developed in such a way that when

---

[26] Wiggins's solution is to require covering concepts to be *sortal* concepts, which serve to pick out individuals. Thus, *mass of water molecules* is not an appropriate covering concept.

[27] David Wiggins, *Identity and Spatio-Temporal Continuity* (Oxford: Clarendon, 1967), 1, 35–6, 50.

[28] P. F. Strawson, *Individuals: An Essay in Descriptive Metaphysics* (London: Methuen, 1959), 97.

we perceive features such as body appearance, body movement, voice, and face we are compelled to experience them as indicative of the presence of a person who has subjectivity.[29]

Evidence for the direct role of neurobiology in person recognition comes from studies involving the stimulation of the amygdala in humans and from various sorts of studies in monkeys. Brothers recorded firing patterns of individual neurons in the amygdalas of macaques while they were observing video clips of social scenes (such as the yawn that males use to signal dominance). These and other results indicate that individual neurons in the amygdala and nearby cortex respond selectively to features such as significant motion, identity of individuals, and particular kinds of interactions taking place between individuals.[30]

The role of neurobiology in enabling us to recognize and participate in the world of persons is further confirmed by patients who, because of brain lesions or other neurological deficits, are unable to use the rules of person language appropriately. For example, patients suffering from misidentification syndrome may attribute one mind to several bodies or perceive a body as having been taken over by an alien mind.[31] Thus, in the normal case our perception of "person" is an automatic and obligatory part of our experience of others – and of ourselves.

There is a longstanding argument in philosophy between those who stake personal identity on spatio-temporal continuity of the body and those who tie it to continuity of memories. There are several reasons for refusing to set these two criteria in opposition to

[29] Leslie A. Brothers, *Friday's Footprint: How Society Shapes the Human Mind* (New York: Oxford, 1997), 4–5.

[30] Leslie A. Brothers, "A Neuroscientific Perspective on Human Sociality," in Robert J. Russell, Nancey Murphy, Theo C. Meyering, and Michael A. Arbib, eds., *Neuroscience and the Person: Scientific Perspectives on Divine Action* (Vatican City State and Berkeley, CA: Vatican Observatory and Center for Theology and the Natural Sciences, 1999), 67–74.

[31] Ibid., 73.

one another. First, as we have just seen, our concept of person essentially involves both a body and a subjectivity. Second, it is an empirical fact (philosophers' bizarre thought experiments notwithstanding) that continuity of memory depends on brain continuity (the physicalist thesis), and thus on some form of bodily continuity.[32]

So can we define physical identity in terms of a *combination* of bodily continuity and memory? I now argue that the combined body–memory criterion is too narrow, in that *memory* does not capture all of what we need in order to secure personal identity.[33] I recount a thought experiment devised by Bernard Williams to show that we need *something* in addition to continuity of memory, although it is difficult to state what that something is.

The first half of Williams's essay reinforces the idea that the memory criterion is the crucial one. Two persons, A and B, enter a machine. When they emerge the A-body-person (that is, the one who has the physical features A had before) has all of B's memories and character traits, and vice versa. The experimenter announces beforehand that after the switch one person will receive $100,000 and the other will be tortured. It is entirely reasonable to expect that, given a choice, A will want the B-body-person to receive the money, rather than be tortured (and vice versa). Williams concludes: "This seems to show that to care about what happens to me in the future is not necessarily to care what happens to *this* body."[34] This and further considerations introduced by Williams seem to confirm the description of the experiment as "changing bodies," and suggest that "the only rational thing to do when confronted with such an experiment would be to identify oneself with one's memories, and so forth, and not with one's body. The philosophical arguments

---

[32] Cf. Wiggins, *Identity and Spatio-Temporal Continuity*, 43.

[33] In the end I propose an account of "same body" that differs from the standard account in that it does not require spatio-temporal continuity or same material constituents.

[34] Bernard Williams, "The Self and the Future," in *Problems of the Self: Philosophical Papers 1956–73* (Cambridge: Cambridge University, 1973), 46–63.

designed to show that bodily identity was at least a necessary condition of personal identity would seem to be just mistaken."[35]

Now consider a different set of cases. You are told that you are going to be tortured tomorrow; you look forward to tomorrow with great apprehension. The person who holds this power over you says, in addition, that between now and then something will be done to you to make you forget everything you now remember. This will not relieve your fear. Then you are told that your memories will be replaced prior to the torture by a complete set of memories from someone else's life. Does this relieve your fear? Williams says that this will not only not relieve your fear but will compound it with fear of mental derangement.

If you are told that your memories will be transferred simultaneously to the other person and that the other will be paid $100,000 we have the same situation with which Williams began his essay, but now our intuitions are reversed: if given a choice, A would want the A-body-person to receive the money and escape the torture.

Williams's thought experiments push us to articulate the sense in which one's consciousness is *more* than a bundle of memories. Recognition of this "more" leads readily to belief in dualism, but it can be understood not as the mind's experience of its (nonmaterial) self, but rather as a product of the integration of various aspects of memory and awareness – a phenomenon that emerges sometime during early childhood. We saw some of the neural prerequisites for a self-concept in the previous chapter (section 4.2). The ability to recognize my conscious self over time is so unproblematic most of the time (e.g. when we wake up in the morning) that it may go unnoticed. An obvious case of failure is the phenomenon of split personality. Its absence is also striking in certain sorts of the misidentification syndrome, in which patients believe they are being transformed into someone else's psychological identity. While we might speculate that this is the effect of reading too

---

[35] Ibid., 51.

much philosophy of mind late at night, such patients show either localized or diffuse brain damage.[36] Schizophrenia often involves the inability to take ownership of one's own thoughts and thus a misattribution of them to God or aliens. Thus, there is some reason for saying that this criterion – I shall call it the continuity-of-consciousness criterion – is, like the memory criterion, contingently connected to the body criterion.

Recognition of oneself as oneself over time and after interruptions of conscious experience may have been presumed to be part of what philosophers have been referring to all along as the memory criterion; I believe Williams has done us a favor by highlighting the distinction. It is particularly helpful in discussing pre- and post-resurrection identity: if God can create a new (transformed) body and provide it with my memories, is that really I? If so, then I shall *know* that I am myself, just as I did this morning when I awoke.

5.2 Theological considerations

I now want to argue that the combined body–memory–consciousness criterion is still too narrow, in that memory and continuity of consciousness together do not capture all of what we need in order to secure personal identity. Given the moral and social character of the kingdom of God, we need to add "same moral character" to our criterion.

Modern thought, following Descartes, has presented an overly cognitivist account of human nature in general and of morality in particular. However, beginning in the 1970s and 1980s, both in Christian ethics and philosophical ethics, there has been a significant movement to return to an understanding of ethics in terms of character. Here the emphasis is not on the rules or principles one ought to follow, but rather on the kind of person one ought to be. These approaches emphasize the development of *virtues*, the

---

[36] Brothers, *Friday's Footprint*, 3–10.

retraining of the *emotions*, and the development of new moral *perceptions*. For example, Alasdair MacIntyre argues that without the acquired capabilities we call virtues, we are not able to achieve the goods intrinsic to social practices.[37] G. Simon Harak's book bears the title *Virtuous Passions*, an oxymoron in the eyes of a purely intellectualist account of morality. His goal is to work out a moral-theological account of the sense of the rightness or wrongness of passions and to consider ways to transform morally blameworthy passions and to foster morally praiseworthy passions.[38] Stanley Hauerwas argues that Christian ethics involves more than making decisions; it is a matter of escaping from self-protective illusions, and of seeing and attending to the world as it really is, in light of its relationship to God.[39]

On the basis of the foregoing, I propose that identity of persons depends as much on *character* identity as it does on memory/consciousness and bodily continuity. That is, a replica or transformed version of my body with all my memories intact would not be I unless she possessed my virtues (or vices), affections, and moral perceptions.[40]

However, it is increasingly clear that, just as the physical and memory criteria are inseparable, so are the character and physical criteria. Virtues are acquired by practice; practice makes stable changes in the strength of relevant neural pathways. Antonio Damasio argues that intelligent action of all sorts is dependent on

---

[37] Alasdair MacIntyre, *After Virtue*, 2nd. edn. (Notre Dame: University of Notre Dame Press, 1984).

[38] G. Simon Harak, *Virtuous Passions: The Formation of Christian Character* (New York: Paulist Press, 1993).

[39] Stanley Hauerwas, "The Significance of Vision," in *Vision and Virtue: Essays in Christian Ethical Reflection* (Notre Dame: University of Notre Dame Press, 1974), 30–47.

[40] Brian Garrett broadens the memory criterion to a "psychological" criterion that includes memory together with other features such as well entrenched beliefs, character, and basic desires. He also argues that the bodily and psychological conditions need to be taken together. See "Personal Identity," in *The Routledge Encyclopedia of Philosophy*, Edward Craig, ed. (London: Routledge, 1998), 7:305–14.

"somatic markers" that reflect one's acquired *affective* relation to the proposed course of action.[41] Perception in general is a bodily process, and moral perception may be hypothesized to depend on the downward efficacy of high-level evaluative processes in reshaping lower-level cognitive propensities – and these changes, too, are recorded in the tuning of neural nets. McClendon argued that Christian ethics cannot be adequately captured except by means of a three-stranded analysis: body ethics, social ethics, and resurrection ethics – his term for ethical analyses that take account of God's action breaking into established biological and social orders. Ethical theories that attend to one or both of the latter will be incomplete and most likely misleading if not balanced by recognition of the drives, needs, and capacities of the *embodied* self.[42]

Another aspect of personal identity is our relationships with others. Philosophers distinguish between internal relations and external relations as follows: internal relations are (partially) constitutive of the related items; external relations are not. Opposing philosophical systems can be constructed by assuming either that all relations are external (logical atomism) or that all are internal (absolute idealism). The sensible position is to recognize that there are some of each. Which or what kind of interpersonal relationships are internal relations – that is, essential to one's identity? It is clear that a great deal of what lasts in the post-resurrection kingdom must be those relationships within the body of Christ that now make us the people we are.

Embodiment is necessary for social life. This would be true even on a dualist account – a body is the soul's only means of relating to other souls. Strawson notes that, if there are disembodied consciousnesses, they are strictly solitary and it is idle speculation for

---

[41] Antonio R. Damasio, *Descartes' Error: Emotion, Reason, and the Human Brain* (New York: G. P. Putnam's Sons, 1994).

[42] James W. McClendon, Jr., *Ethics: Systematic Theology, Volume 1* (Nashville, TN: Abingdon, 1984; rev. edn., 2002).

them as to whether or not there are other consciousnesses.[43] McClendon states that our bodies constitute the very possibility of engagement with one another in this world *or any other*.[44]

Most important, of course, is our relationship to Jesus. Thus, I concur with those who emphasize that God's remembering, recognizing, and relating to me are essential to my post-resurrection identity.

Theological concerns also lead us to consider personal transformation. That is, personal identity is necessary but not sufficient for participation in the post-resurrection kingdom. Keith Ward argues, as I have, that the memory and bodily criteria combined are not sufficient for personal identity – he mentions dispositions, habits, and practices in addition to memory.[45] Ward emphasizes, in addition, that memory needs to be *transformed* since simple vivid reliving of all past experience would undesirably recreate all the suffering and distress of earthly life.

> Memory will be so transformed that suffering is set within a wider context of learning and development, and even earthly joy is relativized by a deeper consciousness of the presence of God. Yet it is important to personal survival that the memories remain, however transformed, so that people who enter into eternal bliss will always know themselves to be the same people who suffered, enjoyed, sinned and repented, learned and developed, on the long journey towards God.[46]

Perfect memory of our evil actions, apart from such a context, might better be described as Hell.

Ward also argues for the possibility of further development of capacities, talents, and dispositions, and for the reshaping of habits

---

[43] Strawson, *Individuals*, 113.

[44] James W. McClendon, Jr., *Doctrine: Systematic Theology, Volume 2* (Nashville, TN: Abingdon Press, 1994), 249. Cf. Neil Gillman, quoted in chapter 1, section 5.3.

[45] Keith Ward, *Religion and Human Nature* (Oxford: Clarendon, 1998), 304.

[46] Ibid., 307; cf. McClendon, *Ethics*, chapter 8.

and skills into more creative forms.[47] An interesting question is the extent to which personal identity can be maintained through the elimination of negative characteristics. We get a sense of how this can happen from narratives of sinners transformed in this life; two classic examples are Augustine's *Confessions* and John Bunyan's *Pilgrim's Progress*.

5.3 Bodily identity

I suggest that one's body should be thought of primarily as that which provides the substrate for all of the personal attributes discussed above: it is that which allows one to be recognized by others; that which bears one's memories; and whose capacities, emotional reactions, and perceptions have been shaped by one's moral actions and experience. It is an empirical fact, in this life, that these essential features are tied to a spatio-temporally continuous material object. Thus, while spatio-temporal continuity is a necessary part of the concept of a material object, I suggest that it is only a contingent part of commonly accepted concepts of the person. That is, all of the personal characteristics as we know them in this life are supported by bodily characteristics and capacities and these bodily capacities happen to belong to a spatio-temporally continuous material object, but there is no reason *in principle* why a body that is numerically distinct but similar in all relevant respects could not support the same personal characteristics.

This recognition allows us to avoid tortuous attempts as in the early church to reconcile resurrection with material continuity.[48] These attempts are based on failure to distinguish the covering concepts of *person* and *material object*, and also fail to recognize that material objects can retain their identity over time despite

---

[47] Ward, *Religion and Human Nature*, 307.

[48] See Carolyn Walker Bynum, *The Resurrection of the Body in Western Christianity, 200–1336* (New York: Columbia University, 1995).

change in the material of which they are composed. My proposal regarding the construal of "same body" also allows for the possibility of a temporal interval between decay of the earthly body and what is then essentially the recreation of a new body out of different "stuff."

5.4 What we know we cannot know

"Stuff" in the previous sentence is used advisedly. While we can know that after the resurrection we shall *be* embodied, and that those bodies will provide the substrate for (or in computer-science terminology, the realization of) the ongoing and endless development of our mental life and moral character, we cannot know anything more of a positive sort about the nature of that stuff. That is, we know that it cannot be the matter with which we are acquainted in the present aeon, both because of the scriptural witness to the *transformation* involved in Jesus' resurrection and because of the fact that the travail of this life is tied so directly to the physics of this world.[49]

Although the New Testament knows nothing of the modern conception of laws of nature, there are passages that can be taken to say that the laws of nature of the present aeon are imperfect, and will be perfected in the Eschaton – fully subjected to the Lordship of Christ. It is now widely accepted that the Pauline concept of the "principalities and powers" (*exousiai* and *dunameis*) refers not to the angels and demons of the medieval worldview, but rather to (largely) social and political powers. (There is nonetheless an echo of the alien gods of Old Testament understanding.) This reinterpretation of the language of the powers serves as a counterargument to the claims that Christianity provides only an individual ethic, and neither an analysis of political power nor a social ethic.

[49] See Robert J. Russell, "Entropy and Evil," *Zygon*, 19:4 (1984): 449–68.

These powers were seen by New Testament authors as subordinate to God – they are God's creatures (Col. 1:15–17), yet they are fallen and rebellious (Eph. 2:1–3; Gal. 4:1–11). Jesus' mission is understood both in the Epistles and Gospels as conflict with and conquest of these powers. In the Epistles, Jesus' victory over the powers is typically represented in summary and proclamatory form as in Colossians 2:15: "He disarmed the principalities and powers and made a public example of them, triumphing over them in him" (RSV). In the Gospels the conflicts are presented in narrative form and the opponents are no longer called "principalities and powers"; rather they are the Herods and Caiphases and Pilates. Wherever Christ's victory is proclaimed, the corrupted reign of the powers is challenged; yet the powers remain in being, for social life is impossible without them. There are hints in the New Testament that the final destiny of all the powers will be not their abolition but their full restoration, "a plan for the fullness of time, to gather up all things in [Christ], things in heaven and things on earth" (Eph. 1:10 NRSV).[50]

The relevance of this material is that while most of the power terms can easily be read as referring to institutional or social realities – thrones, dominions, rulers, powers, the law – there are some oddities, in particular the *stoicheia*. This term occurs seven times in the New Testament. Translations include the four physical elements, the first principles of philosophy, basic religious rituals, the precepts of Jewish law, and the stars conceived as demonic powers.[51] The most common translation in contemporary versions is "elemental spirits." Walter Wink notes that the English term "element" is a formal category that can refer to the most basic constituents or principles of anything; if *stoicheia* is used similarly, this explains the variety of referents, and means that context is crucial for an interpretation. Wink argues that *stoicheia* in Colossians 2:8 ("See to it that no one

---

[50] McClendon, *Ethics*, 173–6.
[51] Walter Wink, *Naming the Powers: The Language of Power in the New Testament* (Philadelphia: Fortress, 1984), 67.

makes a prey of you by philosophical and empty deceit, according to human tradition, according to the elemental spirits of the universe, and not according to Christ") refers to the philosophical search for the first elements or founding principles of the physical universe.[52] In current terminology we could speak of subatomic particles as first elements and the laws of nature as founding principles.

Another hint that the powers include what we would now call the laws of nature comes from McClendon's recognition that in the Gospels Jesus' conflicts with the powers are spelled out in narrative form. In addition to his conflicts with the pharisees and other human powers, there are the demonic forces that sponsor illness and madness. These demons can be cast as actors in the drama, while abstractions such as "authority" and "power" cannot.[53] We now see illness and madness not as the work of demonic forces but as the outcome of the regular working of the laws of nature.

My suggestion, then, is that we can read our concept of the laws of nature *back* into the New Testament texts and so find support for the following theses: (1) The laws of nature of this aeon are God's creatures.[54] (2) Yet, in contrast to early modern understandings of them as perfect expressions of God's will, they are fallen – not in the sense that they once were perfect and then changed, but in the sense that they are meant to be our servants but are instead our masters; they do not enable humankind to live a genuinely free, loving life.[55] (3) Thus, the completion of Christ's work must include a radical transformation of the laws of nature such that they do permit the fullness of human life that God intends.

---

[52] Ibid., 74.   [53] McClendon, *Ethics*, 174.

[54] My use of "laws of nature" is intended to be neutral as to whether the laws in some sense exist and are prescriptive or whether they are simple reflections of regularities in nature. It is interesting that the other powers include both regularities of human social behavior and the Mosaic law, the idea from which the metaphor *laws of nature* was first derived.

[55] Prior to the evolution of life, perhaps the present laws did serve God's purposes perfectly.

We now know a great deal about how natural processes subserve human psychic life. While we can know that, in some manner, glorified bodies support the same (or enhanced) psychic and social capacities, we know that we cannot know *how* this will be in the future. This is because our knowledge of future physical processes is based on projections using current laws of nature. We also know, as argued above, that the laws of nature in the Eschaton (whatever "nature" would then designate) cannot be the same as we have now. Thus, while we might say that table fellowship is so central to the life of the kingdom that we must expect it to continue after the general resurrection, we know in advance that we cannot answer questions about digestion, metabolism, and so forth.

Ludwig Wittgenstein spent his academic life studying the limits of meaningful language; central to his moral vision is the discipline of refraining from speech that goes beyond these limits.[56] So, he once said, while we can speak meaningfully of the hand of God, we cannot speak of God's fingernail.[57] Thus, I conclude that the science–theology dialogue, however fruitful in other areas of theology, must reach a point of silence when we turn to certain matters of eschatology.[58]

6. Conclusion

In these four chapters I have looked at one particular issue regarding human nature: the question of whether humans are purely physical,

---

[56] Brad J. Kallenberg, *Ethics as Grammar: Changing the Postmodern Subject* (Notre Dame: University of Notre Dame Press, 2001).

[57] I have not been able to locate this remark.

[58] For a more extended discussion of topics in this section, see Nancey Murphy, "The Resurrection Body and Personal Identity: Possibilities and Limits of Eschatological Knowledge," in Ted Peters, Robert John Russell, and Michael Welker, eds., *Resurrection: Theological and Scientific Assessments* (Grand Rapids, MI: Eerdmans, 2002), 202–18, from which parts of this section have been excerpted.

or whether there is a non-material component that is essential to our humanness. In my first two chapters I looked at theological and scientific developments, and argued that Christians have nothing to lose and much to gain from recognizing our kinship with the rest of physical creation.

The only danger in adopting a physicalist anthropology, as I argued in my third and fourth chapters, is reductionism. The concept of the soul was first introduced to explain humans' remarkable capacities for reason, morality, spirituality, and free will. If we discard the concept of the soul as unnecessary, this is not to discard higher human capacities, but rather to open ourselves to wonder at the fact that creatures made of the dust of the ground have been raised so high. What, indeed, is man that Thou art mindful of him?

James Dunn's account of Paul's conception of human nature makes a fitting conclusion to this volume:

> In sum, Paul's conception of the human person is of a being who functions within several dimensions. As embodied beings we are social, defined in part by our need for and ability to enter into relationships, not as an optional extra, but as a dimension of our very existence. Our fleshness attests our frailty and weakness as mere humans, the inescapableness of our death, our dependence on satisfaction of appetite and desire, our vulnerability to manipulation of these appetites and desires. At the same time, as rational beings we are capable of soaring to the highest heights of reflective thought. And as experiencing beings we are capable of the deepest emotions and the most sustained motivation. We are living beings, animated by the mystery of life as a gift, and there is a dimension of our being at which we are directly touched by the profoundest reality within and behind the universe. Paul would no doubt say in thankful acknowledgement with the psalmist: "I praise you, for I am fearfully and wonderfully made" (Ps. 139.14).[59]

[59] James D. G. Dunn, *The Theology of the Apostle Paul* (Grand Rapids, MI: Eerdmans, 1998), 78.

My goal here has been to show that our status as embodied creatures in no way contradicts the fact of our sociality; it does not undermine our ability to attain the highest heights of our reflective thought, or our capacity to be sustained by deep emotions and motivations. Least of all is our embodied selfhood an obstacle to being touched by "the profoundest reality within and behind the universe."

Index